D1218501

Landmark Speeches

OF THE AMERICAN CONSERVATIVE MOVEMENT

LANDMARK SPEECHES
A Book Series

Martin J. Medhurst, General Editor

LANDMARK
SPEECHES

OF THE

AMERICAN
CONSERVATIVE
MOVEMENT

Edited by Peter Schweizer and Wynton C. Hall

TEXAS A&M UNIVERSITY PRESS   COLLEGE STATION

The paper used in this book
meets the minimum requirements
of the American National Standard
for Permanence of Paper for
Printed Library Materials, Z39.48-1984.
Binding materials have been chosen for durability.

LIBRARY OF CONGRESS CATALOGING-IN-PUBLICATION DATA

Landmark speeches of the American conservative movement /
edited by Peter Schweizer and Wynton C. Hall.—1st ed.
    p. cm.—(Landmark speeches)
Includes index.
ISBN-13:978-1-58544-584-4 (cloth : alk. paper)
ISBN-10: 1-58544-584-3 (cloth : alk. paper)
ISBN-13: 978-1-58544-598-1 (pbk. : alk. paper)
ISBN-10: 1-58544-598-3 (pbk. : alk. paper)
    1. Conservatism—United States—History—Sources.
2. Speeches, addresses, etc., American.   I. Schweizer, Peter, 1964–
II. Hall, Wynton C., 1976–
JC573.2.U6L36   2007
320.520973—dc22   2006029806

For Rochelle & Katie

CONTENTS

Introduction   1

Whittaker Chambers (1948)   9
   "I Broke Away from the Communist Party"

William F. Buckley Jr. (1950)   14
   "Today We Are Educated Men"

Everett Dirksen (1964)   20
   "The Time Has Come"

Barry Goldwater (1964)   30
   "Extremism in the Defense of Liberty Is No Vice"

Ronald Reagan (1964)   41
   "A Time for Choosing"

Clare Boothe Luce (1978)   55
   "Is the New Morality Destroying America?"

Ronald Reagan (1981)   73
   "The First Inaugural"

Ronald Reagan (1983)   81
   "Evil Empire"

Phyllis Schlafly (1987)   94
   "Child Abuse in the Classroom"

Barbara Bush (1990)   105
   "The Controversy Ends Here"

Newt Gingrich (1995)   111
   "The Contract with America"

George W. Bush (2001)   128
   "Our Mission and Our Moment"

Charles Krauthammer (2004)   139
   "A Unipolar World"

Acknowledgments   161

Index   163

Landmark Speeches

OF THE AMERICAN CONSERVATIVE MOVEMENT

Introduction

What conservatives believe determines how they express their beliefs.

This is true for liberals as well, of course. Both conservatives and liberals want to persuade others. Since they are persuading to different ends, they use different kinds of rhetoric. In both content and form, conservative oratory is distinctive—distinctively rhetorical and characteristically argumentative. What sets it apart is this: pervasive in post–World War II conservatism is an unyielding and vigorous antipathy for relativism in all its varied forms. As Ronald Reagan declared, the conservative banner is one of bold, unmistakable colors, not "pastel shades." This collection of landmark speeches on the American conservative movement demonstrates the rhetorical character and ideological content of contemporary conservatism—an important document for an important force in the nation's political landscape.

At its core, the American conservative movement holds a passion for Absolute Truth (in the classical sense), moral certitude, and an abiding belief in the inverse relationship between personal freedom and federal power: as the latter grows the former is diminished. These tendencies, in fact, are not tendencies at all. Rather, collectively, they represent a unifying current that rushes through each of the speeches contained in this, the first collection of landmark conservative speeches.

We have chosen speeches since 1945 for a simple reason. As George H. Nash wrote in his classic work *The Conservative Intellectual Movement in America,* "In 1945 no articulate, coordinated, self-consciously conservative intellectual force existed in the United States. There were, at most, scattered voices of protest, profoundly pessimistic about the future of their country. Gradually during the first postwar decade these voices multiplied, acquired an audience, and began to generate an intellectual movement."[1] By beginning roughly at the date of origin for modern American conservatism, we can trace the trajectory of conservative rhetoric through time.

Like all anthologies, this one is limited by space and copyright restrictions. Some readers may believe important contributions have been omitted. We agree. Worthy alternatives abound. Still, the oratory assembled represents critical moments in the development of the American conservative movement and thus portrays the movement in its own words.

Speeches were selected based on three criteria. First, for an address to be considered a "landmark" speech it must possess a reach broad enough to impact the movement as a whole. In other words, we interpreted the word "landmark" literally: a speech must have "marked" the conservative "landscape" in some discernible way. Thus, our first criterion was to select speakers with a platform large enough to effect lasting change.

Second, speeches were chosen on the basis of their espousal of conservative principles broadly defined. As noted below, we identified these principles as though laid out in Russell Kirk's important work, *The Conservative Mind*, which the *New York Times* said "gave American conservatives an identity and a genealogy and catalyzed the postwar movement."[2]

Finally, speeches were evaluated with an eye toward their rhetorical artistry and style. Unlike essay writing, which is intended for a reader's eyes, public speaking is intended for an audience's ears. This means that oral discourse demands things prose does not. For this reason, figures like Kirk, Richard M. Weaver, F. A. Hayek, and Irving Kristol, each of whom were enormously important to the growth of the American conservative movement, do not appear. More often than not, their audiences were on the other side of a page, not a podium. Speeches exhibiting, in our judgment, oratorical force, and stylistic refinement received greater attention.

While it is true that conservatives overwhelmingly gravitate toward the Republican Party, selection was not contingent on lifelong party affiliation or ideological labels. Ronald Reagan's switch from the Democratic Party to the GOP is, of course, the most famous example of someone whose conservatism did not reflect a Republican pedigree. Whittaker Chambers, a man who spent much of his life in the Communist Party, similarly came to conservatism later in life. Chambers actually disavowed the label of "conservative," preferring instead to be called "a man of the Right." Moreover, some of the speakers we include, like Barbara Bush, are seldom thought of as leading conservatives. These examples illustrate an important point: the conservative movement's most able spokespersons have often come from unlikely origins.

This diversity also extends to each speaker's rhetorical stratagems as well. The individuals included in this collection were philosophically and politically distinct. Just as there is no one variety of liberalism, so too is there no one "brand" of conservatism. Indeed, the last sixty years have seen American conservatism morph into myriad forms and subgroups like neoconservatism and paleoconservatism, many of which can be heard in the varied voices included in this collection.

While conservative rhetoric is admittedly diverse in both texture and tone, the thirteen speeches contained in this book have several things in common. Specifically, each oration exemplifies the six classic features that Russell Kirk, who as mentioned is widely regarded as one of American conservatism's most influential thinkers and whom Ronald Reagan once called "the prophet of American conservatism," has argued typify conservative thought and speech.

First, conservatives recognize the overarching authority of a higher power. As Kirk puts it, conservatives believe that "political problems, at bottom, are religious and moral problems."[3] To be sure, notable atheists like Ayn Rand have often been associated with conservatism. But generally when considering the question, "Can you be a conservative and despise God and feel contempt for those who believe in Him?" William F. Buckley concludes, "I would say no."[4]

Ronald Reagan's speech at the Annual Convention of the National Association of Evangelicals, March 8, 1983, a speech often called the "Evil Empire" address, is perhaps the clearest example of a modern sitting president espousing a distinctly Christian worldview. Reagan achieves this feat through his invocation of Scripture, references to the works of C. S. Lewis, and the citation of another speaker included in this volume, Whittaker Chambers.

President George W. Bush's speech delivered September 20, 2001—just nine days after the terrorist attacks on the World Trade Center, the Pentagon, and Flight 93—exhibits similar traits. One line in particular drew sharp criticism from some liberals and supporters of separation of church and state: "Freedom and fear, justice and cruelty, have always been at war, and we know that God is not neutral between them."

Second, Kirk says that conservatives hold an "affection for the proliferating variety and mystery of traditional life," which he says engenders a positive, "conservatism of enjoyment."[5] This feature of conservative thought is clearly on display in former First Lady Barbara Bush's Commencement Address at Wellesley College, delivered on June 1, 1990. Recently rated by top rhetoric scholars as the 47th most significant American political speech of the last century, Barbara Bush's humorous, playful address manages to win over a previously hostile crowd—some of whom had protested her appearance—while advancing her thesis that feminist definitions of the "proper" role of womanhood are hypocritically narrow.[6]

Likewise, in 1987, conservative icon Phyllis Schlafly speaks with passion and force at a conference sponsored by the Office of Legal Services of the New York City Board of Education. In her speech Schlafly discusses a series of lawsuits in various states brought by parents and family groups over the content of their children's public school textbooks. The secular humanistic values espoused in these textbooks, Schlafly argues, represent a "direct attack on the First Amendment rights of those who believe that God created us, and that He created a moral law that we should obey. There's nothing neutral about the way these values are taught. The option that we should abide by God's law is never offered."

Third, Kirk argues that conservatives believe that "the only true equality is moral equality," and that "all other attempts at leveling lead to despair, if enforced by positive legislation."[7] Two speeches—one by Republican senator Everett Dirksen arguing for a vote of cloture on the 1964 Civil Rights Act and the other by newly inaugurated Speaker of the House Newt Gingrich—serve as shining examples of Kirk's principle. Dirksen's role in helping the Johnson administration win passage of the bill was critical. By encouraging members of his own party to help defeat southern Democratic opposition to this landmark piece of civil rights legislation, Dirksen's rhetoric persuaded Republicans to continue in the tradition of Lincoln toward the legal instantiation of moral equality.

Speaker Newt Gingrich's inaugural speech picks up the second half of Kirk's mantle. He does this by giving voice to conservative adherence to the law of unintended consequences, which holds that despite the best intentions, governmental intervention almost always exacerbates social ills. Thus, Gingrich contends, "We must replace the welfare state with an opportunity society."

The fourth trait Kirk says typifies conservative thought involves the unwavering belief that individual freedom and private property are inextricably linked. This concept carries with it a catalog of policy implications, including taxation, national security, property rights, self defense, national sovereignty, and freedom from tyranny. In the early postwar era, this tenet of conservatism manifested itself most clearly in an unshakable opposition to socialism and communism. One can feel the urgency of this conviction in the words of Whittaker Chambers, a former member of the Communist Party, as he testified before the House Un-American Activities Committee:

> The Communist Party exists for the specific purpose of overthrowing the Government, at the opportune time, by any and all means. . . . The publicity inseparable from such testimony has darkened, and will no doubt continue to darken, my effort to ingratiate myself in the community of free men. But that is a small price to pay if my testimony helps to make Americans recognize at last they are at grips with a secret, sinister, and enormously powerful force whose tireless purpose is their enslavement.

And nearly a decade and a half later, conservative presidential candidate Barry Goldwater delivered his red meat acceptance address at the 1964 Republican National Convention wherein he reaffirms conservatives' fierce opposition to communist expansion:

> Today, as then, but more urgently and more broadly than then, the task of preserving and enlarging freedom at home and of safeguarding it from the forces of tyranny abroad is great enough to challenge all our resources and to require all our strength.
>
> Anyone who joins us in all sincerity, we welcome. Those who do not care for our cause, we don't expect to enter our ranks in any case. And let our Republicanism, so focused and so dedicated, not be made fuzzy and futile by unthinking and stupid labels.
>
> I would remind you that extremism in the defense of liberty is no vice.

Goldwater's last line produced such thunderous cheers that the second half of his antithesis—the portion meant to temper its strident tone—went largely unnoticed and played into his opponents' theme of portraying Goldwater as dangerous and not to be trusted. (The moderating line: "And let me also remind you that moderation in the pursuit of justice is no virtue.")

Fifth, Kirk contends that conservatives believe that "man must put a control upon his will and his appetite, for conservatives know man to be governed more by emotion than by reason." This reality, Kirk says, leads conservatives to believe that humans must hold their "anarchic impulses" in check.[8] One can see this feature of conservatism in the rhetoric of morality and traditional values that has become so closely associated with American conservatism. Conservatives often meet social issues like abortion, teenage pregnancy and promiscuity, juvenile delinquency, drug abuse, divorce, pornography, and sexual deviance with calls for greater personal responsibility, self-restraint, and self-reliance. In her speech "Is the New Morality Destroying America?" Clare Boothe Luce sounds these themes with clarity and force:

When we examine the "new" sexual morality, what do we discover? We discover that the new sexual morality comes perilously close to being the old universal sexual immorality, whose appearance has again and again portended the decline and fall of past civilizations. The principle on which the new sexual morality is based is sexual selfishness, self-indulgence, and self-gratification. Its credo is I-I-I, Me-Me-Me, and to hell with what others call sex morals.

The final element operative in conservative thought and speech according to Kirk involves the proper velocity of governmental change. "Change may not be salutary reform," writes Kirk, "hasty innovation may be a devouring conflagration, rather than a torch of progress."[9] Here again, the speakers we include prove themselves worthy stewards of the conservative message. A young William F. Buckley, delivering his commencement address at Yale, argues passionately against change for the sake of change: "The retention of the best features of our way of life is the most enlightened and noble of goals." And Ronald Reagan, delivering his 1964 speech in support of Barry Goldwater, decries the expansion of governmental agencies with his trademark wit: "No government ever voluntarily reduces itself in size. Government programs, once launched, never disappear. Actually, a government bureau is the nearest thing to eternal life we'll see on this Earth." Reagan expresses a similar theme in his 1981 inaugural address.

Taken together, these unifying features of conservative thought and speech form a rich rhetorical tradition. The landmark speeches of the American conservative movement have left an indelible imprimatur on the timeline of American oratory—an imprint we believe is worthy of deeper study and appreciation.

Notes

1. George H. Nash, *The Conservative Intellectual Movement in America since 1945* (Wilmington, DE: Intercollegiate Studies Institute, 1996), xv.
2. Patricia Cohen, "Leftist Scholars Look Right at Last, and Find a History," *New York Times*, April 18, 1989, section B, 7.

3. Russell Kirk, *The Conservative Mind: From Burke to Eliot* (Washington, DC: Regnery, 2001), 8.

4. William F. Buckley, "Did You Ever See a Dream Walking?" in *Keeping the Tablets: Modern American Conservative Thought,* ed. William F. Buckley and Charles R. Kesler (New York: Perennial Library, 1988), 28.

5. Kirk, *The Conservative Mind,* 8.

6. Stephen Lucas and Martin J. Medhurst, University of Wisconsin–Madison, "'I Have a Dream' Leads Top 100 Speeches of the Century," December 15, 1999, available online at http://news.wisc.edu/releases/3504.html, accessed July 14, 2006.

7. Russell Kirk, "The Idea of Conservatism," in *Keeping the Tablets: Modern American Conservative Thought,* 44.

8. Kirk, "The Idea of Conservatism," 44.

9. Kirk, *The Conservative Mind,* 9.

Whittaker Chambers

"I Broke Away from the Communist Party"

AUGUST 3, 1948

Testimony before the House Committee

on Un-American Activities

WHITTAKER CHAMBERS WAS BORN Vivian Jay Chambers to a poor family on Long Island, New York, in 1901. Intellectually gifted but troubled, he dropped out of Columbia University and was arrested in his youth for stealing books from the New York Public Library. Passionate about politics at a young age, he was first a fervent supporter of Republican Calvin Coolidge before switching allegiances to the Communist Party in 1925. As a member of the Communist Party, Chambers served as a courier for the Soviet Union, passing information from various agents in the United States. Chambers remained a member of the Communist Party for thirteen years before growing increasingly disillusioned with the party. While Joseph Stalin was purging thousands from the Soviet Party and killing millions, Chambers became frustrated with the American Communist Party's lack of outrage and silent complicity. Finally, in 1938, he denounced the party and proclaimed himself both a Christian and an anticommunist. Over the next fifteen years, he would become one of the most effective critics of communism in the United States at a time of rising national anxiety.

After leaving the party, Chambers joined *Life* magazine and wrote extensively about his experiences in the Communist Party and his conversion to Christianity. Conservative luminaries like William F. Buckley soon embraced Chambers, seeing him as an effective ally in the battle against communism. In an era when both the U.S. Senate and the House of Representatives were conducting hearings on communist subversion in the United States, Chambers became a familiar voice.

His most famous presentation before Congress came in 1948 when he publicly named U.S. governmental officials that he claimed had served as associates during his life as a Soviet subversive. Among those he named was Alger Hiss, a State Department official, friend of President Franklin Delano Roosevelt and Harvard graduate. Hiss denied the accusation, setting off a political firestorm. Much of the Chambers-Hiss dispute got lost in subsequent years because of the ensuing controversies surrounding the techniques and claims of Senator Joseph McCarthy of Wisconsin. However, documents released half a century later from archives in the former Soviet Union tend to confirm Chambers's account that Hiss was indeed working with Soviet intelligence.

Below is Chambers's testimony before the House Un-American Activities Committee. In terms of the development of the American conservative movement, the speech is important on two counts. First, it is one of the first public statements to lay the foundation for American anticommunism, which is one of the pillars of the American conservative movement. Whittaker held that the American Communist Party was not simply a small band of individuals committed to ideas, but that the organization was subservient to a foreign power, namely the Soviet Union.

Second, the speech transformed Chambers into a conservative icon, thus giving him a platform from which to significantly shape the American conservative movement for decades to come. His defection from communism made "conversion" not just a religious term, but a political one as well. Indeed, decades hence, neoconservatives who abandoned the New Left frequently cite Whittaker Chambers as a primary source of inspiration.

Delivered August 3, 1948, in Washington, DC

Almost exactly nine years ago—that is, two days after Hitler and Stalin signed their pact—I went to Washington and reported to the authorities what I knew about the infiltration of the United States Government by Communists. For years international communism, of which the United States Communist Party is an integral part, had been in a state of undeclared war with this Republic. With the Hitler-Stalin pact, that war reached a new stage. I regarded my action in going to the government as a simple act of war, like the shooting of an armed enemy in combat. At that moment in history, I was one of the few men on this side of the battle who could perform this service. I had joined the Communist Party in 1924. No one recruited me. I had become convinced that the society in which we live, western civilization, had reached a crisis, of which the First World War was the military expression, and that it was doomed to collapse or revert to barbarism. I did not understand the causes of the crisis or know what to do about it. But I felt that, as an intelligent man, I must do something. In the writings of Karl Marx I thought that I had found "the explanation of the historical and economic causes." In the writings of Lenin I thought I had found the answer to the question, "What to do?" In 1937 I repudiated Marx's doctrines and Lenin's tactics. Experience and the record had convinced me that communism is a form of totalitarianism, that its triumph means slavery to men wherever they fall under its sway, and spiritual night to the human mind and soul. I resolved to break with the Communist Party at whatever risk to my life or other tragedy to myself or my family. Yet, so strong is the hold which the insidious evil of communism secures on its disciples that I could still say to someone at the time: "I know that I am leaving the winning side for the losing side, but it is better to die on the losing side than to live under communism."

For a year I lived in hiding, sleeping by day and watching through the night with gun or revolver within easy reach. That was what underground communism could do to one man in the peaceful United States in the year 1938. I had sound reason for supposing that the Communists might try to kill me. For a number of years I had myself served in the under-ground, chiefly in Washington, D.C. The heart of my report to the United States Government consisted of a description of the apparatus to which I was attached. It was an underground organization of the United States Communist Party developed, to the best of my knowledge, by Harold Ware, one of the sons of the Communist leader known as "Mother Bloor." I knew it at its top level, a group of seven or so men, from among whom in later years certain members of Miss Bentley's organization were apparently recruited. The head of the underground group at the time I knew it was Nathan Witt, an attorney for the National Labor Relations Board. Later, Tohn Abt became the leader. Lee Pressman was also a member of this group, as was Alger Hiss, who, as a member of the State Department, later organized the conferences at Dumbarton Oaks, San Francisco, and the United States side of the Yalta Conference.

The purpose of this group at that time was not primarily espionage. Its original purpose was the Communist infiltration of the American Government. But espionage was certainly one of its eventual objectives. Let no one be surprised at this statement. Disloyalty is a matter of principle with every member of the Communist Party. The Communist Party exists for the specific purpose of overthrowing the Government; at the opportune time, by any and all means; and each of its members, by the fact that he is a member, is dedicated to this purpose.

It is 10 years since I broke away from the Communist Party. During that decade I have sought to live an industrious and God-fearing life. At the same time I have fought communism constantly by act and written word. I am proud to appear before this committee. The publicity inseparable from such testimony has darkened, and will no doubt continue to darken, my effort to integrate myself in the community of free men. But that is a small price to pay if my testimony helps to make Americans recognize at last that they are at grips with a secret, sinister, and enormously powerful force whose tireless purpose is their enslavement. At the same time, I should like, thus publicly, to call upon all ex-Communists who have not yet declared themselves, and all men within the Communist Party whose better instincts have not yet been corrupted and crushed by it, to aid in this struggle while there is still time to do so.

William F. Buckley Jr.

"Today We Are Educated Men"

JUNE 11, 1950

The Class Day Oration at Yale University

"THE GODFATHER OF American conservatism." "The architect of the modern conservative movement." "The intellectual father of modern conservatism." These are just some of the phrases often used to describe William F. Buckley Jr. Indeed, it is hard for one to imagine the American conservative movement without him. As Ronald Reagan once put it, "Bill Buckley is perhaps the most influential journalist and intellectual in our era—he changed our country, indeed our century."

William F. Buckley, or WFB as he is commonly referred to within conservative circles, was born on November 24, 1925, in New York City. One of ten children, his parents were both devout Roman Catholics. His father was a wealthy oil man. Despite growing up on the family's estate in Sharon, Connecticut, Buckley adopted as his first language the Spanish used by the Mexican nannies who largely raised him. It would not be until the young WFB attended day school in London that he would learn to speak English.

In 1944, Buckley served a short stint in the Army before working briefly for the CIA and graduating from Yale University. At the age of twenty-five, Buckley would publish his first and most famous book, *God and Man at Yale*. A polemic against Leftist hegemony in higher education, the book's success ignited Buckley's meteoric rise to the top of the literary world.

On November 19, 1955, Buckley published the first issue of the periodical with which he is most closely associated, *National Review* (*NR*). The magazine, which has never posted a financial profit, remains an essential gathering place for American conservatives. Virtually every notable conservative cites *NR* as an important part of his or her intellectual pilgrimage. As Buckley famously wrote in the magazine's inaugural issue, *National Review* "stands athwart history, yelling Stop, at a time when no one is inclined to do so."

Ten years after the publication of *NR*'s first issue, Buckley ran a largely symbolic campaign for mayor of New York City under the banner of the Conservative Party ticket for which he received 13.4 percent of the vote. Later, WFB created the debate-style television show *Firing Line*, which he hosted for more than thirty years. Viewers quickly became fans of his commanding oratory, stately cadence, and the sheer breadth of his intellectual prowess.

Buckley also remains one of the most prolific voices from the political Right. As *Boston Globe* columnist Jeff Jacoby notes, WFB has written "35 nonfiction books, 15 books of fiction, 79 book reviews, 56 introductions or forewords to books written by others, 227 obituary essays, 800-plus editorials or other articles in *National Review*, 350 articles in periodicals other than *National Review*, and more than 4,000 newspaper columns."[1] He has also been the recipient of numerous awards, including the Presidential Medal of Freedom, which he received in 1991.

In his personal life, Buckley has gained a reputation as being somewhat of a Renaissance man—he is a lover of words and language, an avid snow skier and sailor, and has even mastered the harpsichord. He and his wife Patricia married in 1950 and are the parents of Christopher Buckley, an accomplished writer in his own right. But the year of their matrimonial marks another landmark; for this was the same year WFB would deliver a speech that launched his public career.

In "Today We Are Educated Men," Buckley presages the broadsides he would later unload in *God and Man at Yale*; namely, that change for change's sake is folly; that the moral and religious virtues of our ancestors are worth preserving; and that institutions of higher education mustn't become a monolithic voice of the political Left, but rather should foster true intellectual diversity. In so doing, a young WFB takes the first of many steps toward establishing himself as both a leading public figure and one of the premiere spokesmen of the American conservative movement.

Delivered June 11, 1950, in New Haven, Connecticut

A year ago, the orator for the class of 1949 stood here and told his classmates that the troubles of the United States in particular and of Western democracy in general were attributable to the negativism of our front against Communism. His was not a lone voice jarring smug opinion in mid-twentieth-century America. Rather he is part of the swelling forefront of men and women who are raising a hue and a cry for what they loosely call positivism, by which they mean bold new measures, audacious steps forward, a reorientation towards those great new horizons and that Brave New World.

It is natural at this point to realize that (although we must be very careful how we put it) we are, as Yale men, privileged members of our society, and to us falls the responsibility of leadership in this great new positivist movement. For we had had a great education, and our caps and gowns weigh heavy upon us as we face our responsibilities to mankind.

All of us here have been exposed to four years' education in one of the most enlightened and advanced liberal-arts colleges in the world. Here we can absorb the last word in most fields of academic endeavor. Here we find the headquarters of a magazine devoted exclusively to metaphysics, and another devoted entirely to an analysis of French existentialism. And here, for better or for worse, we have been jolted forcefully from any preconceived judgments we may have had when we came. Here we can find men who will tell us that Jesus Christ was the greatest fraud that history has known. Here we can find men who will tell us that morality is an anachronistic conception, rendered obsolete by the advances of human thought. From neo-Benthamites at Yale we can learn that laws are a sociological institution, to be wielded to facilitate the sacrosanct will of the enlightened minority.

Communism is a real force to cope with only because of the deficiencies of democracy. Our fathers, who worked to send us to Yale, their fathers and their fathers, who made Yale and the United States, were hardworking men, shrewd men, and performed a certain economic service, but they were dreadfully irresponsible, y'know, in view of today's enlightenment.

And so it goes: two and two make three, the shortest distance between two points is a crooked line, good is bad and bad is good, and from this morass we are to extract a workable, enlightened synthesis to govern our thoughts and our actions, for today we are educated men.

Nothing, it is true, is healthier than honest scrutiny, with maybe even a little debunking thrown in. When a dean tells us that our task is to go out and ennoble mankind, we nod our heads and wonder whether the opening in the putty-knife factory or in the ball-bearing works will pay more. When we are told that Lincoln was totally unconcerned with politics, we might ponder the occasion in 1863 when he could not focus his attention on the questions of a distinguished visitor because he was terribly worried over what Republican to appoint postmaster of Chicago. In 1913 Charles Beard wrote his Economic Interpretation of the Constitution. It was banned in seven state universities and brought almost nationwide ostracism for the author. Today a study of this analysis is a prerequisite to a doctoral degree in American history.

Certainly civilization cannot advance without freedom of inquiry. This fact is self-evident. What seems equally self-evident is that in the process of history certain immutable truths have been revealed and discovered and that their value is not subject to the limitations of time and space. The probing, the relentless debunking, has engendered a skepticism that threatens to pervade and atrophy all our values. In apologizing for our beliefs and our traditions we have bent over backwards so far that we have lost our balance, and we see a topsy-turvy world and we say topsy-turvy things, such as that the way to beat Communism is by making our democracy better. What a curious self-examination! Beat the Union of Soviet Socialist Republics by making America socialistic. Beat atheism by denying God. Uphold individual freedom by denying natural rights. We neglect to say to the Communist, "In the name of heaven look at what we now have. Your standards don't interest us." As Emerson threatened to say to the obstreperous government tax collector, "If you pursue, I will slit your throat, sir."

The credo of the so-called positivists is characterized by the advocacy of change. Republicanism, on the other hand, is negativism because conservatives believe that America has grown and has prospered, has put muscle on her bones, by rewarding initiative and industry, by conceding to her citizens not only the right and responsibilities of self-government, but also the right and responsibilities of self-care, of individually earned security. The role of the so-called conservative is a difficult one. A starry-eyed young man, nevertheless aggressive in his wisdom, flaunting the badge of custodian of the common man, approaches our neat, sturdy white house and tells us we must destroy it, rebuild it of crystallized cold cream, and paint it purple. "But we like it the way it is," we retort feebly.

"Rip 'er down! This is a changing world."

Is our effort to achieve perspective all the more difficult by virtue of our having gone to Yale? In many respects it is, because the university does not actively aid us in forming an enlightened synthesis. That job is for us to perform: to reject those notions that do not square with the enlightenment that should be ours as moral, educated men, beneficiaries of centuries of historical experience. Yale has given us much. Not least is an awesome responsibility to withstand her barrage, to emerge from her halls with both feet on the ground, with a sane head and a reinforced set of values. If our landing is accomplished, we are stronger men for our flight.

Keenly aware, then, of the vast deficiencies in American life today—the suffering, the injustice, the want—we must nevertheless spend our greatest efforts, it seems to me, in preserving the framework that supports the vaster bounties that make our country an oasis of freedom and prosperity. Our concern for deficiencies in America must not cause us to indict the principles that have allowed our country, its faults notwithstanding, to tower over the nations of the world as a citadel of freedom and wealth. With what severity and strength we can muster, we must punch the gasbag of cynicism and skepticism, and thank providence for what we have and must retain. Our distillation of the ideas, concepts, and theories expounded at Yale must serve to enhance our devotion to the good in what we have, to reinforce our allegiance to our principles, to convince us that our outlook is positive: that the retention of the best features of our way of life is the most enlightened and noble of goals. Insofar as the phrase "For God, for Country, and for Yale" is meaningful, we need not be embarrassed to mean "For God as we know him, for country as we know it, and for Yale as we have known her."

Notes

1. Jeff Jacoby, "There's No Stopping Bill Buckley," *Boston Globe,* July 1, 2004, online and available at: http://www.boston.com/news/globe/editorial_opinion/oped/articles/2004/07/01/theres_no_stopping_bill_buckley/, accessed June 12, 2006.

Everett Dirksen

"The Time Has Come"

JUNE 10, 1964

A Call for Cloture on the Civil Rights Act of 1964

THAT EVERETT MCKINLEY DIRKSEN would become one of the Republican Party's leading lights should have come as no surprise. His parents, Johann and Antje, both German immigrants, decided to name their sons after famous GOP figures: Everett bore the middle name McKinley; his twin brother was named after Republican Speaker of the House Thomas Reed; and his eldest brother became Benjamin Harrison Dirksen.

He was born January 4, 1896. "I come of immigrant German stock," said Dirksen, "My mother stood on Ellis Island as a child of 17, with a tag around her neck directing that she be sent to Pekin, Illinois."[1] And so it was that "the pride of Pekin," Everett McKinley Dirksen, would launch his political career in the land of Lincoln.

Dirksen attended the University of Minnesota before enlisting in the Army where he was commissioned overseas as a 2nd Lieutenant. Upon his return to Pekin, he participated in the Pekin Centennial play, "A Thousand Years Ago." There, he would meet Louella Carver whom he would marry in 1927. After an initial failed run for a U.S. House seat, in 1932 Dirksen was elected to his first of eight consecutive terms. By 1950, he would make the leap to the U.S. Senate where he would be elected as Senate minority leader, a position he held until his death in 1969.

Over the span of his nearly four decades in public service, Everett Dirksen gained a reputation as "the Senate's most practiced and professional orator."[2] And it would be these skills, combined with his unsurpassed knowledge of Senate rules, that helped halt a five-month-long filibuster—the longest in the history of the U.S. Senate—and thus paved the way for passage of the landmark Civil Rights Act of 1964. Ironically, the Illinois Republican—carrying the proequality mantle of Lincoln—would come to the aid of Democrats and their president, Lyndon Baines Johnson.

Southern Democratic senators had been intent on killing the legislation; breaking their filibuster seemed all but impossible. A vote of cloture (which would end a filibuster and allow a final vote to be taken) required two-thirds of Senate support. In 1964, Democrats accounted for exactly two-thirds (sixty-seven members) of the U.S. Senate. The problem for the Johnson Administration was that twenty-one of the sixty-seven Democratic senators staunchly opposed the bill. To break the southern Democratic logjam, LBJ and the remaining pro–civil rights Democrats would need twenty-two of the Senate's thirty-three Republicans to join their ranks.[3]

The night before his historic address in support of cloture, the sixty-eight-year-old senator typed his speech on twelve pages of Senate stationery. Motivating him was the memory of his young, immigrant mother standing on a windswept Ellis Island. "Our family had opportunities in Illinois, and the essence of what we're trying to do in the civil rights bill is to see that others have opportunities in this country," he would later explain.[4]

Following Dirksen's speech and passage of the bill, Democratic Majority Leader Mike Mansfield said, "This is his [Dirksen] finest hour. The Senate, the whole country is in debt to the Senator from Illinois." *Time* magazine agreed, and put him on the cover the following week. In that issue, *Time* wrote that Dirksen's speech delivered just fifteen minutes before the vote on cloture was taken "more than anyone else's had made a favorable cloture vote likely."[5] Indeed, without Everett Dirksen's leadership, the Civil Rights Act of 1964 might never have been passed.

Delivered June 10, 1964, in Washington, DC
Mr. President, it is a year ago this month that the late President Kennedy sent his civil rights bill and message to the

Congress. For two years, we had been chiding him about failure to act in this field. At long last, and after many conferences, it became a reality.

After nine days of hearings before the Senate Judiciary Committee, it was referred to a subcommittee. There it languished and the administration leadership finally decided to await the House bill.

In the House it traveled an equally tortuous road. But at long last, it reached the House floor for action. It was debated for 64 hours; 155 amendments were offered; 34 were approved. On February 10, 1964, it passed the House by a vote of 290 to 130. That was a 65-percent vote.

It was messaged to the Senate on February 17 and reached the Senate calendar on February 26. The motion to take up and consider was made on March 9. That motion was debated for sixteen days and on March 26 by a vote of 67 to 17 it was adopted.

It is now four months since it passed the House. It is three and a half months since it came to the Senate calendar. Three months have gone by since the motion to consider was made. We have acted on one intervening motion to send the bill back to the Judiciary Committee and a vote on the jury trial amendment. That has been the extent of our action.

Sharp opinions have developed. Incredible allegations have been made. Extreme views have been asserted. The mail volume has been heavy. The bill has provoked many long-distance telephone calls, many of them late at night or in the small hours of the morning. There has been unrestrained criticism about motives. Thousands of people have come to the Capitol to urge immediate action on an unchanged House bill.

For myself, I have had but one purpose and that was the enactment of a good, workable, equitable, practical bill having due regard for the progress made in the civil rights field at the state and local level.

I am no Johnnie-come-lately in this field. Thirty years ago, in the House of Representatives, I voted on anti-poll tax and anti-lynching measures. Since then, I have sponsored or co-sponsored scores of bills dealing with civil rights.

At the outset, I contended that the House bill was imperfect and deficient. That fact is now quite generally conceded. But the debate continued. The number of amendments submitted increased. They now number nearly four hundred. The stalemate continued. A backlog of work piled up. Committees could not function normally. It was an unhappy situation and it was becoming a bit intolerable.

It became increasingly evident that to secure passage of a bill in the Senate would require cloture and a limitation on debate. Senate aversion to cloture is traditional. Only once in thirty-five years has cloture been voted. But the procedure for cloture is a standing rule of the Senate. It grew out of a filibuster against the Armed Ship bill in 1917 and has been part of the standing rules of the Senate for forty-seven years. To argue that cloture is unwarranted or unjustified is to assert that in 1917, the Senate adopted a rule which it did not intend to use when circumstances required or that it was placed in the rulebook only as to be repudiated. It was adopted as an instrument for action when all other efforts failed.

Today the Senate is stalemated in its efforts to enact a civil rights bill, one version of which has already been approved by the House by a vote of more than 2 to 1. That the Senate wishes to act on a civil rights bill can be divined from the fact that the motion to take up was adopted by a vote of 67 to 17.

There are many reasons why cloture should be invoked and a good civil rights measure enacted.

First. It is said that on the night he died, Victor Hugo wrote in his diary, substantially this sentiment:

"Stronger than all the armies is an idea whose time has come."

The time has come for equality of opportunity in sharing in government, in education, and in employment. It will not be stayed or denied. It is here.

The problem began when the Constitution makers permitted the importation of persons to continue for another twenty years. That problem was to generate the fury of civil strife seventy-five years later. Out of it was to come the Thirteenth Amendment ending servitude, the Fourteenth Amendment to provide equal protection of the laws and dual citizenship, the Fifteenth Amendment to prohibit government from abridging the right to vote.

Other factors had an impact. Two and three-quarter million young Negroes served in World Wars I, II, and Korea. Some won the Congressional Medal of Honor and the Distinguished Service Cross. Today they are fathers and grandfathers. They brought back impressions from countries where no discrimination existed. These impressions have been transmitted to children and grandchildren. Meanwhile, hundreds of thousands of colored have become teachers and professors, doctors and dentists, engineers and architects, artists and actors, musicians and technicians. They have become status minded. They have sensed inequality. They are prepared to make the issue. They feel that the time has come for the idea of equal opportunity. To enact the pending measure by invoking cloture is imperative.

Second. Years ago, a professor who thought he had developed an incontrovertible scientific premise submitted it to his faculty associates. Quickly they picked it apart. In agony he cried out, "Is nothing eternal?" To this one of his associates replied, "Nothing is eternal except change."

Since the act of 1875 on public accommodations and the Supreme Court decision of 1883 which struck it down, America has changed. The population then was 45 million. Today it is 190 million. In the Pledge of Allegiance to the Flag we intone, "One nation, under God." And so it is. It is an integrated nation. Air, rail, and highway transportation make it so. A common language makes it so. A tax pattern which applies equally to white and nonwhite makes it so. Literacy makes it so. The mobility provided by eighty million autos makes it so. The accommodations laws in thirty-four states and the District of Columbia makes it so. The fair employment practice laws in thirty states make it so. Yes, our land has changed since the Supreme Court decision of 1883.

As Lincoln once observed:

"The occasion is piled high with difficulty and we must rise with the occasion. As our case is new, so we must think anew and act anew. We must first disenthrall ourselves and then we shall save the Union."

To my friends from the South, I would refresh you on the words of a great Georgian named Henry W. Grady. On December 22, 1886, he was asked to respond to a toast to the new South at the New England society dinner. His words were dramatic and explosive. He began his toast by saying:

"There was a South of slavery and secession—that South is dead."

There is a South of union and freedom—that South thank God is living, breathing, growing every hour.

America grows. America changes. And on the civil rights issue we must rise with the occasion. That calls for cloture and for the enactment of a civil rights bill.

Third. There is another reason—our covenant with the people. For many years, each political party has given major consideration to a civil rights plank in its platform. Go back and reexamine our pledges to the country as we sought the suffrage of the people and for a grant of authority to manage and direct their affairs. Were these pledges so much campaign stuff or did we mean it? Were these promises on civil rights but idle words for vote-getting purposes or were they a covenant meant to be kept? If all this was mere pretense, let us confess the sin of hypocrisy now and vow not to delude the people again.

To you, my Republican colleagues, let me refresh you on the words of a great American. His name is Herbert Hoover. In his day he was reviled and maligned. He was castigated and calumniated. But today his views and his judgment stand vindicated at the bar of history. In 1952 he received a volcanic welcome as he appeared before our national convention in Chicago. On that occasion he commented on the Whig party, predecessor of the Republican party, and said:

"The Whig party temporized, compromised upon the issue of freedom for the Negro."

That party disappeared. It deserved to disappear. Shall the Republican party receive or deserve any better fate if it compromises upon the issue of freedom for all men?

To those who have charged me with doing a disservice to my party because of my interest in the enactment of a good civil rights bill—and there have been a good many who have made that charge—I can only say that our party found its faith in the Declaration of Independence in which a great Democrat, Jefferson by name, wrote the flaming words:

"We hold these truths to be self-evident that all men are created equal."

That has been the living faith of our party. Do we forsake this article of faith, now that equality's time has come? Or do we stand up for it and insure the survival of our party and its ultimate victory? There is no substitute for a basic and righteous idea. We have a duty—a firm duty—to use the instruments at hand—namely, the cloture rule—to bring about the enactment of a good civil rights bill.

Fourth. There is another reason why we dare not temporize with the issue which is before us. It is essentially moral in character. It must be resolved. It will not go away. Its time has come. Nor is it the first time in our history that an issue with moral connotations and implications has swept away the resistance, the fulminations, the legalistic speeches, the ardent but dubious arguments, the lamentations and the thought patterns of an earlier generation and pushed forward to fruition.

More than sixty years ago came the first efforts to secure federal pure food and drug legislation. The speeches made on this floor against this intrusion of federal power sound fantastically incredible today. But it would not be stayed. Its time had come and since its enactment, it has been expanded and strengthened in nearly every Congress.

When the first efforts were made to ban the shipment of goods in interstate commerce made with child labor, it was regarded as quite absurd. But all the trenchant editorials, the bitter speeches, the noisy onslaughts were swept aside as this limitation on the shipment of goods made with sweated child labor moved on to fulfillment. Its time had come.

More than eighty years ago came the first efforts to establish a civil service and merit system to cover federal employees. The proposal was ridiculed and drenched with sarcasm. Some of the sharpest attacks on the proposal were made on this very Senate floor. But the bullet fired by a disappointed office seeker in 1880 which took President Garfield's life was the instrument of destiny which placed the Pendleton Act on the federal statute books in 1883. It was an idea whose time had come.

When the New York legislature placed a limit of ten hours per day and six days per week upon the bakery workers in that State, this act was struck down by the U.S. Supreme Court. But in due time came the eight-hour day and the forty-hour week and how broadly accepted this concept is today. Its time had come.

More than sixty years ago, the elder La Follette thundered against the election of U.S. senators by the state legislatures. The cry was to get back to the people and to first principles. On this Senate floor, senators sneered at his efforts and even left the chamber to show their contempt. But fifty years ago, the Constitution was amended to provide for the direct election of senators. Its time had come.

Ninety-five years ago came the first endeavor to remove the limitation on sex in the exercise of the franchise. The comments made in those early days sound unbelievably ludicrous. But on and on went the effort and became the Nineteenth Amendment to the Constitution. Its time had come.

When the eminent Joseph Choate appeared before the Supreme Court to assert that a federal income tax statute was unconstitutional and communistic, the Court struck down the work of Congress. Just twenty years later in 1913 the power of Congress to lay and collect taxes on incomes became the Sixteenth Amendment to the Constitution itself.

These are but some of the things touching closely the affairs of the people which were met with stout resistance, with shrill and strident cries of radicalism, with strained legalisms, with anguished entreaties that the foundations of the Republic were being rocked. But an inexorable moral force which operates in the domain of human affairs swept these efforts aside and today they are accepted as parts of the social, economic and political fabric of America.

Pending before us is another moral issue. Basically it deals with equality of opportunity in exercising the franchise, in securing an education, in making a livelihood, in enjoying the mantle of protection of the law. It has been a long, hard furrow and each generation must plow its share. Progress was made in 1957 and 1960. But the furrow does not end there. It requires the implementation provided by the substitute measure which is before us. And to secure that implementation requires cloture.

Let me add one thought to these observations. Today is an anniversary. It is in fact the one-hundredth anniversary of the nomination of Abraham Lincoln for a second term for the presidency on the Republican ticket. Two documents became the blueprints for his life and his conduct. The first was the Declaration of Independence which proclaimed the doctrine that all men are created equal. The second was the Constitution, the preamble to which began with the words:

"We, the people . . . do ordain and establish this Constitution for the United States of America."

These were the articles of his superb and unquenchable faith. Nowhere and at no time did he more nobly reaffirm that faith than at Gettysburg 101 years ago when he spoke of "a new nation, conceived in liberty and dedicated to the proposition that all men are created equal."

It is to take us further down that road that a bill is pending before us. We have a duty to get that job done. To do it will require cloture and a limitation on debate as provided by a standing rule of the Senate which has been in being for nearly fifty years. I trust we shall not fail in that duty.

That, from a great Republican, thinking in the frame of equality of opportunity—and that is all that is involved in this bill.

To those who have charged me with doing a disservice to my party—and there have been many—I can only say that our party found its faith in the Declaration of Independence, which was penned by a great Democrat, Thomas Jefferson by name. There he wrote the great words:

"We hold these truths to be self-evident, that all men are created equal."

That has been the living faith of our party. Do we forsake this article of faith, now that the time for our decision has come?

There is no substitute for a basic ideal. We have a firm duty to use the instrument at hand; namely, the cloture rule, to bring about the enactment of a good civil rights bill.

I appeal to all senators. We are confronted with a moral issue. Today let us not be found wanting in whatever it takes by way of moral and spiritual substance to face up to the issue and to vote cloture.

Notes

1. "The Covenant," *Time* magazine, June 19, 1964; Everett McKinley Dirksen, *The Education of a Senator* (Urbana: University of Illinois Press, 1998).

2. "The Covenant," *Time.*

3. "Everett McKinley Dirksen's Finest Hour: June 10, 1964," *Peoria Journal Star,* June 10, 2004.

4. "The Covenant," *Time.*

5. Ibid.

Barry Goldwater

"Extremism in the Defense of Liberty Is No Vice"

JULY 16, 1964

Presidential Acceptance Speech at the

Republican National Convention

BARRY M. GOLDWATER was born in 1909 to a merchant family in Arizona. After attending the Staunton Military Academy, he attended the University of Arizona for one year before joining the family business. During the Second World War he enlisted in the U.S. Army Air Corps, serving in the Pacific and then India. For several decades following the war, he was a member of the Reserves, reaching the rank of Brigadier General in the Air Force Reserve.

Arizona culture shaped Goldwater's politics. Distrustful of government and a staunch individualist, he embraced the doctrine of limited government as a touchstone of his political beliefs. It was this philosophy that he carried with him first to the Phoenix City Council and then to the U.S. Senate in 1952.

In 1964 Goldwater sought and won the Republican nomination for president. His campaign represented a significant turning point for the Republican Party. Long dominated by moderates who believed that an active and expanding federal government was a fact of life, Goldwater sought to remake the GOP by emphasizing his libertarian political philosophy. Although in favor of civil rights, Goldwater opposed federal government legislation on civil rights that he viewed as a usurpation of states' rights. He was a moderate on social issues like abortion, but he opposed efforts by federal courts or the Congress to impose those views on states.

Goldwater's acceptance speech at the Republican National Convention in San Francisco, California, is remarkable when viewed in the light of contemporary politics. Far from compromising in an effort to broaden his political base, Goldwater stuck firmly to his ideological convictions. It is often said that while Goldwater lost the 1964 election to Lyndon Johnson soundly, he launched a conservative revolution that remade the GOP and, in the end, paved the way for his chief campaign spokesman, Ronald Reagan.

Delivered July 16, 1964, in San Francisco, California
My good friend and great Republican, Dick Nixon, and your charming wife, Pat; my running mate, that wonderful Republican who has served us so well for so long, Bill Miller and his wife, Stephanie; to Thurston Morton who's done such a commendable job in chairmaning this Convention; to Mr. Herbert Hoover, who I hope is watching; and to that great American and his wife, General and Mrs. Eisenhower; to my own wife, my family, and to all of my fellow Republicans here assembled, and Americans across this great Nation.

From this moment, united and determined, we will go forward together, dedicated to the ultimate and undeniable greatness of the whole man. Together we will win. I accept your nomination with a deep sense of humility. I accept, too, the responsibility that goes with it, and I seek your continued help and your continued guidance. My fellow Republicans, our cause is too great for any man to feel worthy of it. Our task would be too great for any man, did he not have with him the hearts and the hands of this great Republican Party, and I promise you tonight that every fiber of my being is consecrated to our cause; that nothing shall be lacking from the struggle that can be brought to it by enthusiasm, by devotion, and plain hard work.

In this world no person, no Party can guarantee anything, but what we can do and what we shall do is to deserve victory, and victory will be ours.

The good Lord raised this mighty Republic to be a home for the brave and to flourish as the land of the free. Not to stagnate in the swampland of collectivism, not to cringe before the bullying of communism.

Now, my fellow Americans, the tide has been running against freedom. Our people have followed false prophets. We must, and we shall, return to proven ways. Not because they are old, but because they are true. We must, and we shall, set the tides running again in the cause of freedom. And this party, with its every action, every word, every breath, and every heartbeat, has but a single resolve, and that is freedom made orderly for this Nation by our constitutional government; freedom under a government limited by the laws of nature and of nature's God; freedom balanced so that order lacking liberty will not become the slavery of the prison cell; balanced so that liberty lacking order will not become the license of the mob and of the jungle.

Now, we Americans understand freedom. We have earned it; we have lived for it, and we have died for it. This Nation and its people are freedom's model in a searching world. We can be freedom's missionaries in a doubting world. But, ladies and gentlemen, first we must renew freedom's mission in our own hearts and in our own homes.

During four futile years, the administration which we shall replace has distorted and lost that vision. It has talked and talked and talked and talked the words of freedom, but it has failed and failed and failed in the works of freedom.

Now, failures cement the wall of shame in Berlin. Failures blot the sands of shame at the Bay of Pigs. Failures mark the slow death of freedom in Laos. Failures infest the jungles of Vietnam. And failures haunt the houses of our once great alliances and undermine the greatest bulwark ever erected by free nations—the NATO community. Failures proclaim lost leadership, obscure purpose, weakening will, and the risk of inciting our sworn enemies to new aggressions and to new excesses.

And because of this administration we are tonight a world divided; we are a Nation becalmed. We have lost the brisk pace of diversity and the genius of individual creativity. We are plodding along at a pace set by centralized planning, red tape, rules without responsibility, and regimentation without recourse.

Rather than useful jobs in our country, our people have been offered bureaucratic "make work"; rather than moral leadership, they have been given bread and circuses. They have been given spectacles, and, yes, they've even been given scandals.

Tonight, there is violence in our streets, corruption in our highest offices, aimlessness amongst our youth, anxiety among our elders, and there's a virtual despair among the many who look beyond material success for the inner meaning of their lives. And where examples of morality should be set, the opposite is seen. Small men, seeking great wealth or power, have too often and too long turned even the highest levels of public service into mere personal opportunity.

Now, certainly, simple honesty is not too much to demand of men in government. We find it in most. Republicans demand it from everyone. They demand it from everyone no matter how exalted or protected his position might be. Now the growing menace in our country tonight, to personal safety, to life, to limb and property, in homes, in churches, on the playgrounds, and places of business, particularly in our great cities, is the mounting concern, or should be, of every thoughtful citizen in the United States.

Security from domestic violence, no less than from foreign aggression, is the most elementary and fundamental purpose of any government, and a government that cannot fulfill this purpose is one that cannot long command the loyalty of its citizens.

History shows us, it demonstrates that nothing, nothing prepares the way for tyranny more than the failure of public officials to keep the streets safe from bullies and marauders.

Now, we Republicans see all this as more, much more, than the result of mere political differences or mere political mistakes. We see this as the result of a fundamentally and absolutely wrong view of man, his nature, and his destiny. Those who seek to live your lives for you, to take your liberties in return for relieving you of yours, those who elevate the state and downgrade the citizen must see ultimately a world in which earthly power can be substituted for Divine Will, and this Nation was founded upon the rejection of that notion and upon the acceptance of God as the author of freedom.

Now those who seek absolute power, even though they seek it to do what they regard as good, are simply demanding the right to enforce their own version of heaven on earth. They, and let me remind you, they are the very ones who always create the most hellish tyrannies. Absolute power does corrupt, and those who seek it must be suspect and must be opposed. Their mistaken course stems from false notions, ladies and gentlemen, of equality. Equality, rightly understood, as our founding fathers understood it, leads to liberty and to the emancipation of creative differences. Wrongly understood, as it has been so tragically in our time, it leads first to conformity and then to despotism.

Fellow Republicans, it is the cause of Republicanism to resist concentrations of power, private or public, which enforce such conformity and inflict such despotism. It is the cause of Republicanism to ensure that power remains in the hands of the people. And, so help us God, that is exactly what a Republican President will do with the help of a Republican Congress.

It is further the cause of Republicanism to restore a clear understanding of the tyranny of man over man in the world at large. It is our cause to dispel the foggy thinking which avoids hard decisions in the delusion that a world of conflict will somehow mysteriously resolve itself into a world of harmony, if we just don't rock the boat or irritate the forces of aggression—and this is hogwash.

It is further the cause of Republicanism to remind ourselves, and the world, that only the strong can remain free, that only the strong can keep the peace.

Now, I needn't remind you, or my fellow Americans regardless of party, that Republicans have shouldered this hard responsibility and marched in this cause before. It was Republican leadership under Dwight Eisenhower that kept the peace, and passed along to this administration the mightiest arsenal for defense the world has ever known. And I needn't remind you that it was the strength and the unbelievable will of the Eisenhower years that kept the peace by using our strength, by using it in the Formosa Straits and in Lebanon and by showing it courageously at all times.

It was during those Republican years that the thrust of Communist imperialism was blunted. It was during those years of Republican leadership that this world moved closer, not to war, but closer to peace, than at any other time in the last three decades.

And I needn't remind you—but I will—that it's been during Democratic years that our strength to deter war has stood still, and even gone into a planned decline. It has been during Democratic years that we have weakly stumbled into conflict, timidly refusing to draw our own lines against aggression, deceitfully refusing to tell even our people of our full participation, and tragically, letting our finest men die on battlefields, unmarked by purpose, unmarked by pride or the prospect of victory.

Yesterday, it was Korea. Tonight, it is Vietnam. Make no bones of this. Don't try to sweep this under the rug. We are at war in Vietnam. And yet the President, who is the Commander-in-Chief of our forces, refuses to say, mind you, whether or not the objective over there is victory. And his Secretary of Defense continues to mislead and misinform the American people, and enough of it has gone by.

And I needn't remind you—but I will—it has been during Democratic years that a billion persons were cast into Communist captivity and their fate cynically sealed.

Today in our beloved country we have an administration

which seems eager to deal with communism in every coin known—from gold to wheat, from consulates to confidences, and even human freedom itself.

Now the Republican cause demands that we brand communism as the principal disturber of peace in the world today. Indeed, we should brand it as the only significant disturber of the peace, and we must make clear that until its goals of conquest are absolutely renounced and its relations with all nations tempered, communism and the governments it now controls are enemies of every man on earth who is or wants to be free.

Now, we here in America can keep the peace only if we remain vigilant and only if we remain strong. Only if we keep our eyes open and keep our guard up can we prevent war. And I want to make this abundantly clear: I don't intend to let peace or freedom be torn from our grasp because of lack of strength or lack of will—and that I promise you, Americans.

I believe that we must look beyond the defense of freedom today to its extension tomorrow. I believe that the communism which boasts it will bury us, will, instead, give way to the forces of freedom. And I can see in the distant and yet recognizable future the outlines of a world worthy of our dedication, our every risk, our every effort, our every sacrifice along the way. Yes, a world that will redeem the suffering of those who will be liberated from tyranny. I can see—and I suggest that all thoughtful men must contemplate—the flowering of an Atlantic civilization, the whole of Europe reunified and freed, trading openly across its borders, communicating openly across the world.

Now, this is a goal far, far more meaningful than a moon shot.

It's a truly inspiring goal for all free men to set for themselves during the latter half of the twentieth century.

I can also see—and all free men must thrill to—the events of this Atlantic civilization joined by its great ocean highway to the United States. What a destiny! What a destiny can be ours to stand as a great central pillar linking Europe, the Americas, and the venerable and vital peoples and cultures of the Pacific. I can see a day when all the Americas, North and South, will be linked in a mighty system, a system in which the errors and misunderstandings of the past will be submerged one by one in a rising tide of prosperity and interdependence. We know that the misunderstandings of centuries are not to be wiped away in a day or wiped away in an hour. But we pledge that human sympathy—what our neighbors to the South call an attitude of "simpatico"—no less than enlightened self-interest will be our guide.

And I can see this Atlantic civilization galvanizing and guiding emergent nations everywhere.

Now I know this freedom is not the fruit of every soil. I know that our own freedom was achieved through centuries, by unremitting efforts of brave and wise men. And I know that the road to freedom is a long and a challenging road. And I know also that some men may walk away from it, that some men resist challenge, accepting the false security of governmental paternalism.

And I pledge that the America I envision in the years ahead will extend its hand in health, in teaching and in cultivation, so that all new nations will be at least encouraged—encouraged!—to go our way, so that they will not wander down the dark alleys of tyranny or the dead-end streets of collectivism.

My fellow Republicans, we do no man a service by hiding freedom's light under a bushel of mistaken humility.

I seek an America proud of its past, proud of its ways, proud of its dreams, and determined actively to proclaim them. But our example to the world must, like charity, begin at home.

In our vision of a good and decent future, free and peaceful, there must be room, room for deliberation of the energy and the talent of the individual; otherwise our vision is blind at the outset.

We must assure a society here which, while never abandoning the needy or forsaking the helpless, nurtures incentives and opportunities for the creative and the productive.

We must know the whole good is the product of many single contributions.

And I cherish a day when our children once again will restore as heroes the sort of men and women who, unafraid and undaunted, pursue the truth, strive to cure disease, subdue and make fruitful our natural environment and produce the inventive engines of production, science, and technology.

This Nation, whose creative people have enhanced this entire span of history, should again thrive upon the greatness of all those things which we, we as individual citizens, can and should do. And during Republican years, this again will be a nation of men and women, of families proud of their role, jealous of their responsibilities, unlimited in their aspirations—a Nation where all who can will be self-reliant.

We Republicans see in our constitutional form of government the great framework which assures the orderly but dynamic fulfillment of the whole man, and we see the whole man as the great reason for instituting orderly government in the first place.

We see in private property and in economy based upon and fostering private property, the one way to make government a durable ally of the whole man, rather than his determined enemy. We see in the sanctity of private property the only durable foundation for constitutional government in a free society. And beyond that, we see, in cherished diversity of ways, diversity of thoughts, of motives and accomplishments. We don't seek to lead anyone's life for him. We only seek to secure his rights, guarantee him opportunity to strive, with government performing only those needed and constitutionally sanctioned tasks which cannot otherwise be performed.

We Republicans seek a government that attends to its inherent responsibilities of maintaining a stable monetary and fiscal climate, encouraging a free and a competitive economy and enforcing law and order. Thus do we seek inventiveness, diversity, and creative difference within a stable order, for we Republicans define government's role where needed at many, many levels—preferably, though, the one closest to the people involved.

Our towns and our cities, then our counties, then our states, then our regional compacts—and only then, the national government. That, let me remind you, is the ladder of liberty, built by decentralized power. On it also we must have balance between the branches of government at every level.

Balance, diversity, creative difference: These are the elements of the Republican equation. Republicans agree heartily to disagree on many, many of their applications, but we have never disagreed on the basic fundamental issues of why you and I are Republicans.

This is a Party. This Republican Party is a Party for free men, not for blind followers, and not for conformists.

In fact, in 1858 Abraham Lincoln said this of the Republican Party—and I quote him, because he probably could have said it during the last week or so: "It was composed of strange, discordant, and even hostile elements"—end of the quote—in 1858.

Yet all of these elements agreed on one paramount objective: To arrest the progress of slavery, and place it in the course of ultimate extinction.

Today, as then, but more urgently and more broadly than then, the task of preserving and enlarging freedom at home and of safeguarding it from the forces of tyranny abroad is great enough to challenge all our resources and to require all our strength.

Anyone who joins us in all sincerity, we welcome. Those who do not care for our cause, we don't expect to enter our ranks in any case. And let our Republicanism, so focused and so dedicated, not be made fuzzy and futile by unthinking and stupid labels.

I would remind you that extremism in the defense of liberty is no vice.

(Thank you. Thank you. Thank you. Thank you. Thank you.)

And let me remind you also that moderation in the pursuit of justice is no virtue.

Why the beauty of the very system we Republicans are pledged to restore and revitalize, the beauty of this Federal system of ours is in its reconciliation of diversity with unity. We must not see malice in honest differences of opinion, and no matter how great, so long as they are not inconsistent with the pledges we have given to each other in and through our Constitution.

Our Republican cause is not to level out the world or make its people conform in computer-regimented sameness. Our Republican cause is to free our people and light the way for liberty throughout the world.

Ours is a very human cause for very humane goals.

This Party, its good people, and its unquenchable devotion to freedom, will not fulfill the purposes of this campaign, which we launch here and now, until our cause has won the day, inspired the world, and shown the way to a tomorrow worthy of all our yesteryears.

I repeat, I accept your nomination with humbleness, with pride, and you and I are going to fight for the goodness of our land.

Thank you.

Ronald Reagan

"A Time for Choosing"

October 27, 1964

Televised Campaign Speech in Support of Barry Goldwater

RONALD REAGAN WAS BORN to a poor Illinois family in 1911. The son of an alcoholic father and religious mother, he attended Eureka College where he studied economics. After college he worked for several radio stations in Iowa before moving to Hollywood to enter the motion picture business.

Although he made a comfortable living starring in films such as *King's Row* and *The Cattle Queen of Montana*, Reagan never achieved A-level star status. Following the Second World War, he devoted an increasing amount of his time to labor union activities, particularly the Screen Actors Guild.

As a child, Reagan idolized Democratic president Franklin Delano Roosevelt. But his political views began to change as he entered adulthood. Following the outbreak of the cold war and the experience of paying what he considered high income taxes, Reagan became increasingly conservative. He began reading works by Whittaker Chambers and struck up a friendship with Senator Barry Goldwater of Arizona. (Nancy Reagan's father, who lived in Arizona, was friendly with Goldwater.) By the 1950s when Reagan had become a spokesman for General Electric, he was a full-fledged conservative who took his message of individual responsibility, limited government, anticommunism, and deregulation to audiences around the country.

In 1962, Reagan's political migration was complete: he switched his party registration from Democrat to Republican. Two years later, as the presidential campaign of Barry Goldwater floundered, he was asked by several prominent Goldwater supporters to give a nationally televised speech to make the case for the candidate. Below is that speech, titled "A Time for Choosing." Reagan's address received national acclaim as millions listened on television. While the speech failed to get Goldwater elected president, it put Reagan on the national political map. Indeed, two years later, Reagan would successfully seek the governorship of California.

The speech is significant because, along with Goldwater's acceptance speech, it signifies the shift of the Republican Party away from its moderate, northeastern roots and toward a Western, more ideologically charged philosophy. While Reagan's speech sounds some of the same alarms as Goldwater's address, it differs in its decidedly optimistic tone, which stood in sharp contradistinction to the Arizona senator's more pessimistic rhetoric.

Delivered October 27, 1964, in Los Angeles, California

Thank you very much. Thank you and good evening. The sponsor has been identified, but unlike most television programs, the performer hasn't been provided with a script. As a matter of fact, I have been permitted to choose my own words and ideas regarding the choice that we face in the next few weeks.

I have spent most of my life as a Democrat. I recently have seen fit to follow another course. I believe that the issues confronting us cross party lines. Now, one side in this campaign has been telling us that the issues of this election are the maintenance of peace and prosperity. The line has been used, "We've never had it so good."

But I have an uncomfortable feeling that this prosperity isn't something on which we can base our hopes for the future. No nation in history has ever survived a tax burden that reached a third of its national income. Today, 37 cents out of every dollar earned in this country is the tax collector's share, and yet our government continues to spend $17 million dollars a day more than the government takes in. We haven't balanced our budget 28 out of the last 34 years. We've raised our debt limit three times in the last twelve months, and now our national debt is one and a half times bigger than all the combined debts of all the nations in the world. We have $15 billion in gold in our treasury—we don't own an ounce. Foreign dollar claims are $27.3 billion, and we have just had announced that the dollar of 1939 will now purchase 45 cents in its total value.

As for the peace that we would preserve, I wonder who among us would like to approach the wife or mother whose husband or son has died in South Vietnam and ask them if they think this is a peace that should be maintained indefinitely. Do they mean peace, or do they mean we just want to be left in peace? There can be no real peace while one American is dying some place in the world for the rest of us. We are at war with the most dangerous enemy that has ever faced mankind in his long climb from the swamp to the stars, and it has been said if we lose that war, and in doing so lose this way of freedom of ours, history will record with the greatest astonishment that those who had the most to lose did the least to prevent its happening. Well, I think it's time we ask ourselves if we still know the freedoms that were intended for us by the Founding Fathers.

Not too long ago two friends of mine were talking to a Cuban refugee, a businessman who had escaped from Castro, and in the midst of his story one of my friends turned to the other and said, "We don't know how lucky we are." And the Cuban stopped and said, "How lucky you are! I had someplace to escape to." In that sentence he told us the entire story. If we lose freedom here, there is no place to escape to. This is the last stand on Earth.

And this idea that government is beholden to the people, that it has no other source of power except to sovereign people, is still the newest and most unique idea in all the long history of man's relation to man. This is the issue of this election. Whether we believe in our capacity for self-government or whether we abandon the American revolution and confess that a little intellectual elite in a far-distant capital can plan our lives for us better than we can plan them ourselves.

You and I are told increasingly that we have to choose between a left or right, but I would like to suggest that there is no such thing as a left or right. There is only an up or down—up to a man's age-old dream, the ultimate in individual freedom consistent with law and order—or down to the ant heap totalitarianism, and regardless of their sincerity, their humanitarian motives, those who would trade our freedom for security have embarked on this downward course.

In this vote-harvesting time, they use terms like the "Great Society," or as we were told a few days ago by the President, we must accept a "greater government activity in the affairs of the people." But they have been a little more explicit in the past and among themselves—and all of the things that I now will quote have appeared in print. These are not Republican accusations. For example, they have voices that say "the Cold War will end through acceptance of a not undemocratic socialism." Another voice says that the profit motive has become outmoded, it must be replaced by the incentives of the welfare state; or our traditional system of individual freedom is incapable of solving the complex problems of the 20th century. Senator Fulbright has said at Stanford University that the Constitution is outmoded. He referred to the president as our moral teacher and our leader, and he said he is hobbled in his task by the restrictions in power imposed on him by this antiquated document. He must be freed so that he can do for us what he knows is best.

And Senator Clark of Pennsylvania, another articulate spokesman, defines liberalism as "meeting the material needs of the masses through the full power of centralized government." Well, I for one resent it when a representative of the people refers to you and me—the free man and woman of this country—as "the masses." This is a term we haven't applied to ourselves in America. But beyond that, "the full power of centralized government"—this was the very thing the Founding Fathers sought to minimize. They knew that governments don't control things. A government can't control the economy without controlling people. And they know when a government sets out to do that, it must use force and coercion to achieve its purpose. They also knew, those Founding Fathers, that outside of its legitimate functions, government does nothing as well or as economically as the private sector of the economy.

Now, we have no better example of this than the government's involvement in the farm economy over the last 30 years. Since 1955, the cost of this program has nearly doubled. One-fourth of farming in America is responsible for 85 percent of the farm surplus. Three-fourths of farming is out on the free market and has known a 21 percent increase in the per capita consumption of all its produce. You see, that one-fourth of farming is regulated and controlled by the federal government. In the last three years we have spent $43 in the feed grain program for every bushel of corn we don't grow.

Senator Humphrey last week charged that Barry Goldwater as President would seek to eliminate farmers. He should do his homework a little better, because he will find out that we have had a decline of 5 million in the farm population under these government programs. He will also find that the Democratic administration has sought to get from Congress an extension of the farm program to include that three-fourths that is now free. He will find that they have also asked for the right to imprison farmers who wouldn't keep books as prescribed by the federal government. The Secretary of Agriculture asked for the right to seize farms through condemnation and resell them to other individuals. And contained in that same program was a provision that would have allowed the federal government to remove 2 million farmers from the soil.

At the same time, there has been an increase in the Department of Agriculture employees. There is now one for every 30 farms in the United States, and still they can't tell us how 66 shiploads of grain headed for Austria disappeared without a trace and Billie Sol Estes never left shore.

Every responsible farmer and farm organization has

repeatedly asked the government to free the farm economy, but who are farmers to know what is best for them? The wheat farmers voted against a wheat program. The government passed it anyway. Now the price of bread goes up; the price of wheat to the farmer goes down.

Meanwhile, back in the city, under urban renewal the assault on freedom carries on. Private property rights are so diluted that public interest is almost anything that a few government planners decide it should be. In a program that takes for the needy and gives to the greedy, we see such spectacles as in Cleveland, Ohio, a million-and-a-half-dollar building completed only three years ago must be destroyed to make way for what government officials call a "more compatible use of the land." The President tells us he is now going to start building public housing units in the thousands where heretofore we have only built them in the hundreds. But FHA and the Veterans Administration tell us that they have 120,000 housing units they've taken back through mortgage foreclosures. For three decades, we have sought to solve the problems of unemployment through government planning, and the more the plans fail, the more the planners plan. The latest is the Area Redevelopment Agency.

They have just declared Rice County, Kansas, a depressed area. Rice County, Kansas, has two hundred oil wells, and the 14,000 people there have over $30 million on deposit in personal savings in their banks. When the government tells you you're depressed, lie down and be depressed.

We have so many people who can't see a fat man standing beside a thin one without coming to the conclusion that the fat man got that way by taking advantage of the thin one. So they are going to solve all the problems of human misery through government and government planning. Well, now, if government planning and welfare had the answer and they've had almost 30 years of it, shouldn't we expect government to almost read the score to us once in a while? Shouldn't they be telling us about the decline each year in the number of people needing help? The reduction in the need for public housing?

But the reverse is true. Each year the need grows greater, the program grows greater. We were told four years ago that 17 million people went to bed hungry each night. Well, that was probably true. They were all on a diet. But now we are told that 9.3 million families in this country are poverty-stricken on the basis of earning less than $3,000 a year. Welfare spending is 10 times greater than in the dark depths of the Depression. We are spending $45 billion on welfare. Now do a little arithmetic, and you will find that if we divided the $45 billion up equally among those 9 million poor families, we would be able to give each family $4,600 a year, and this added to their present income should eliminate poverty! Direct aid to the poor, however, is running only about $600 per family. It would seem that someplace there must be some overhead.

So now we declare "war on poverty," or "you, too, can be a Bobby Baker!" Now, do they honestly expect us to believe that if we add $1 billion to the $45 million we are spending . . . one more program to the 30-odd we have—and remember, this new program doesn't replace any, it just duplicates existing programs—do they believe that poverty is suddenly going to disappear by magic? Well, in all fairness I should explain that there is one part of the new program that isn't duplicated. This is the youth feature. We are now going to solve the dropout problem, juvenile delinquency, by reinstituting something like the old CCC camps, and we are going to put our young people in camps, but again we do some arithmetic, and we find that we are going to spend each year just on room and board for each young person that we help $4,700 a year! We can send them to Harvard for $2,700! Don't get me wrong. I'm not suggesting that Harvard is the answer to juvenile delinquency.

But seriously, what are we doing to those we seek to help? Not too long ago, a judge called me here in Los Angeles. He told me of a young woman who had come before him for a divorce. She had six children, was pregnant with her seventh. Under his questioning, she revealed her husband was a laborer earning $250 a month. She wanted a divorce so that she could get an $80 raise. She is eligible for $330 a month in the Aid to Dependent Children Program. She got the idea from two women in her neighborhood who had already done that very thing.

Yet anytime you and I question the schemes of the do-gooders, we are denounced as being against their humanitarian goals. They say we are always "against" things, never "for" anything.

Well, the trouble with our liberal friends is not that they are ignorant, but that they know so much that isn't so.

We are for a provision that destitution should not follow unemployment by reason of old age, and to that end we have accepted Social Security as a step toward meeting the problem.

But we are against those entrusted with this program when they practice deception regarding its fiscal shortcomings, when they charge that any criticism of the program means that we want to end payments to those who depend on them for livelihood. They have called it insurance to us in a hundred million pieces of literature. But then they appeared before the Supreme Court and they testified that it was a welfare program. They only use the term "insurance" to sell it to the people. And they said Social Security dues are a tax for the general use of the government, and the government has used that tax. There is no fund, because Robert Byers, the actuarial head, appeared before a congressional committee and admitted that Social Security as of this moment is $298 billion in the hole. But he said there should be no cause for worry because as long as they have the power to tax, they could always take away from the people whatever they needed to bail them out of trouble! And they are doing just that.

A young man, 21 years of age, working at an average salary, his Social Security contribution would, in the open market, buy him an insurance policy that would guarantee $220 a month at age 65. The government promises $127. He could live it up until he is 31 and then take out a policy that would pay more than Social Security. Now, are we so lacking in business sense that we can't put this program on a sound basis so that people who do require those payments will find that they can get them when they are due . . . that the cupboard isn't bare? Barry Goldwater thinks we can.

At the same time, can't we introduce voluntary features that would permit a citizen who can do better on his own to be excused upon presentation of evidence that he had made provisions for the non-earning years? Should we allow a widow with children to work, and not lose the benefits supposedly paid for by her deceased husband? Shouldn't you and I be allowed to declare who our beneficiaries will be under these programs, which we cannot do? I think we are for telling our senior citizens that no one in this country should be denied medical care because of a lack of funds. But I think we are against forcing all citizens, regardless of need, into a compulsory government program, especially when we have such examples, as announced last week, when France admitted that their Medicare program was now bankrupt. They've come to the end of the road.

In addition, was Barry Goldwater so irresponsible when he suggested that our government give up its program of deliberate planned inflation so that when you do get your Social Security pension, a dollar will buy a dollar's worth, and not 45 cents worth?

I think we are for an international organization, where the nations of the world can seek peace. But I think we are against subordinating American interests to an organization that has become so structurally unsound that today you can muster a two-thirds vote on the floor of the General Assembly among the nations that represent less than 10 percent of the world's population. I think we are against the hypocrisy of assailing our allies because here and there they cling to a colony, while we engage in a conspiracy of silence and never open our mouths about the millions of people enslaved in Soviet colonies in the satellite nation.

I think we are for aiding our allies by sharing of our material blessings with those nations which share in our fundamental beliefs, but we are against doling out money government to government, creating bureaucracy, if not socialism, all over the world. We set out to help 19 countries. We are helping 107. We spent $146 billion. With that money, we bought a $2 million yacht for Haile Selassie. We bought dress suits for Greek undertakers, extra wives for Kenyan government officials. We bought a thousand TV sets for a place where they have no electricity. In the last six years, 52 nations have bought $7 billion worth of our gold, and all 52 are receiving foreign aid from this country.

No government ever voluntarily reduces itself in size. Government programs, once launched, never disappear. Actually, a government bureau is the nearest thing to eternal life we'll ever see on this Earth. Federal employees number 2.5 million, and federal, state, and local, one out of six of the nation's work force is employed by the government. These proliferating bureaus with their thousands of regulations have cost us many of our constitutional safeguards. How many of us realize that today federal agents can invade a man's property without a warrant? They can impose a fine without a formal hearing, let alone a trial by jury, and they can seize and sell his property in auction to enforce the payment of that fine. In Chico County, Arkansas, James Wier over planted his rice allotment. The government obtained a $17,000 judgment, and a U.S. marshal sold his 950-acre farm at auction. The government said it was necessary as a warning to others to make the system work. Last February 19th at the University of Minnesota, Norman Thomas, six-time candidate for President on the Socialist Party ticket, said, "If Barry Goldwater became President, he would stop the advance of socialism in the United States." I think that's exactly what he will do.

As a former Democrat, I can tell you Norman Thomas isn't the only man who has drawn this parallel to socialism with the present administration. Back in 1936, Mr. Democrat himself, Al Smith, the great American, came before the American people and charged that the leadership of his party was taking the party of Jefferson, Jackson, and Cleveland down the road under the banners of Marx, Lenin, and Stalin.

And he walked away from his party, and he never returned to the day he died, because to this day, the leadership of that party has been taking that party, that honorable party, down the road in the image of the labor socialist party of England.

Now it doesn't require expropriation or confiscation of private property or business to impose socialism on a people. What does it mean whether you hold the deed or the title to your business or property if the government holds the power of life and death over that business or property? Such machinery already exists. The government can find some charge to bring against any concern it chooses to prosecute. Every businessman has his own tale of harassment. Somewhere a perversion has taken place. Our natural, inalienable rights are now considered to be a dispensation of government, and freedom has never been so fragile, so close to slipping from our grasp as it is at this moment. Our Democratic opponents seem unwilling to debate these issues. They want to make you and I believe that this is a contest between two men; that we are to choose just between two personalities.

Well, what of this man that they would destroy? And in destroying, they would destroy that which he represents, the ideas that you and I hold dear. Is he the brash and shallow and trigger-happy man they say he is? Well, I have been privileged to know him "when." I knew him long before he ever dreamed of trying for high office, and I can tell you personally I have never known a man in my life I believe so incapable of doing a dishonest or dishonorable thing.

This is a man who in his own business, before he entered politics, instituted a profit-sharing plan, before unions had ever thought of it. He put in health and medical insurance for all his employees. He took 50 percent of the profits before taxes and set up a retirement program, a pension plan for all his employees. He sent checks for life to an employee who was ill and couldn't work. He provided nursing care for the children of mothers who work in the stores. When Mexico was ravaged by floods from the Rio Grande, he climbed in his airplane and flew medicine and supplies down there.

An ex-GI told me how he met him. It was the week before Christmas during the Korean War, and he was at the Los Angeles airport trying to get a ride home to Arizona for Christmas, and he said that there were a lot of servicemen there and no seats available on the planes. Then a voice came over the loudspeaker and said, "Any men in uniform wanting a ride to Arizona, go to runway such-and-such," and they went down there, and there was this fellow named Barry Goldwater sitting in his plane. Every day in the weeks before Christmas, all day long, he would load up the plane, fly to Arizona, fly them to their homes, then fly back over to get another load.

During the hectic split-second timing of a campaign, this is a man who took time out to sit beside an old friend who was dying of cancer. His campaign managers were understandably impatient, but he said, "There aren't many left who care what happens to her. I'd like her to know I care." This is a man who said to his 19-year-old son, "There is no foundation like the rock of honesty and fairness, and when you begin to build your life upon that rock, with the cement of the faith in God that you have, then you have a real start." This is not a man who could carelessly send other people's sons to war. And that is the issue of this campaign that makes all of the other problems I have discussed academic, unless we realize that we are in a war that must be won.

Those who would trade our freedom for the soup kitchen of the welfare state have told us that they have a utopian solution of peace without victory. They call their policy "accommodation." And they say if we only avoid any direct confrontation with the enemy, he will forget his evil ways and learn to love us. All who oppose them are indicted as warmongers. They say we offer simple answers to complex problems. Well, perhaps there is a simple answer—not an easy answer—but simple.

If you and I have the courage to tell our elected officials that we want our national policy based upon what we know in our hearts is morally right. We cannot buy our security, our freedom from the threat of the bomb by committing an immorality so great as saying to a billion now in slavery behind the Iron Curtain, "Give up your dreams of freedom because to save our own skin, we are willing to make a deal with your slave masters." Alexander Hamilton said, "A nation which can prefer disgrace to danger is prepared for a master, and deserves one." Let's set the record straight. There is no argument over the choice between peace and war, but there is only one guaranteed way you can have peace—and you can have it in the next second—surrender.

Admittedly there is a risk in any course we follow other than this, but every lesson in history tells us that the greater risk lies in appeasement, and this is the specter our well-meaning liberal friends refuse to face—that their policy of accommodation is appeasement, and it gives no choice between peace and war, only between fight and surrender. If we continue to accommodate, continue to back and retreat, eventually we have to face the final demand—the ultimatum. And what then? When Nikita Khrushchev has told his people he knows what our answer will be? He has told them that we are retreating under the pressure of the Cold War, and someday when the time comes to deliver the ultimatum, our surrender will be voluntary because by that time we will have weakened from within spiritually, morally, and economically. He believes this because from our side he has heard voices pleading for "peace at any price" or "better Red than dead," or as one commentator put it, he would rather "live on his knees than die on his feet." And therein lies the road to war, because those voices don't speak for the rest of us.

You and I know and do not believe that life is so dear and peace so sweet as to be purchased at the price of chains and slavery. If nothing in life is worth dying for, when did this be-gin—just in the face of this enemy? Or should Moses have told the children of Israel to live in slavery under the pharaohs? Should Christ have refused the cross? Should the patriots at Concord Bridge have thrown down their guns and refused to fire the shot heard 'round the world? The martyrs of history were not fools, and our honored dead who gave their lives to stop the advance of the Nazis didn't die in vain. Where, then, is the road to peace? Well, it's a simple answer after all.

You and I have the courage to say to our enemies, "There is a price we will not pay." There is a point beyond which they must not advance. This is the meaning in the phrase of Barry Goldwater's "peace through strength." Winston Churchill said that "the destiny of man is not measured by material computation. When great forces are on the move in the world, we learn we are spirits—not animals." And he said, "There is something going on in time and space, and beyond time and space, which, whether we like it or not, spells duty."

You and I have a rendezvous with destiny. We will preserve for our children this, the last best hope of man on Earth, or we will sentence them to take the last step into a thousand years of darkness.

We will keep in mind and remember that Barry Goldwater has faith in us. He has faith that you and I have the ability and the dignity and the right to make our own decisions and determine our own destiny.

Thank you very much.

Clare Boothe Luce

"Is the New Morality Destroying America?"

Toward a Moral Renaissance

IN THE PANTHEON OF FIGURES associated with the American conservative movement, perhaps none has lived a more eclectic life than playwright, journalist, congresswoman, and ambassador Clare Boothe Luce. Born on April 10, 1903, in New York City, Luce inherited her parents' flair for the theatrical. Her father, William Franklin Boothe, was a pit orchestra violinist. Her mother, the former Anna Clara Snyder, was a chorus girl. At the age of eight, Luce's parents separated, forcing her to be raised in "genteel poverty." But her modest financial status would be short-lived, as she would soon soar to the top of the economic ladder. Indeed, Luce, a woman known for her glamour and rapier wit, would always take pride in poking holes in the pretenses of wealth and power.[1]

Following her divorce from her abusive millionaire husband, George Tuttle Brokaw, a man twenty-three years her senior, Luce was awarded enough money—$425,000 plus education expenses for her daughter, Anne Clare Brokaw—to never work again. But Luce, a woman never accused of sloth, had other plans. She became an editor at *Vogue* and *Vanity Fair* before turning her attention to writing plays.

She would later meet and marry Henry R. Luce, publisher of *Time, Fortune, Sports Illustrated,* and *Life,* a magazine that was reportedly her idea.[2] Luce continued writing plays, two of which,

"The Women" and "Kiss the Boys Goodbye," enjoyed critical acclaim and financial success at the box office.

By 1943, the strong-willed and outspoken Luce was ready to set her sites on another challenge—Congress. An ardent anticommunist and New Deal critic, Luce, a Republican, managed to unseat the Democratic incumbent by 7,000 votes. Having coined famous epigrams like "No good deed goes unpunished," Luce's skill as a playwright lent vivacity to her oratory. Moreover, in a male-dominated era, Luce's unique brand of feminism stood out. As she put it, "Thoughts have no sex."

President Dwight D. Eisenhower agreed, apparently. After campaigning for him in 1952, Ike tapped Luce to serve in his cabinet as secretary of labor. When Luce declined the president's offer, the former general wouldn't take no for an answer and instead named her ambassador to Italy. While in this position, her staunch anticommunist position made her a lightning rod for the political Left. For example, while speaking about the relationship between intellectuals and communism, Luce once said, "Communism is the opiate of the intellectuals with no cure except as a guillotine might be called a cure for dandruff."

Yet Luce's greatest threat came not from her political opponents, but from the strange illness that befell her while in Italy. The cause: arsenic-laced paint dust that had fallen from the ceiling of her bedroom.

Luce regained her health and in 1964 entertained a short-lived run for the United States Senate. In the years that followed, she removed herself from public life but remained a strong advocate for conservative principles. In 1981, President Reagan appointed her to the President's Foreign Intelligence Advisory Board. And by 1983, Clare Boothe Luce received a fitting ending to her Horatio Alger–like life when she was awarded the Presidential Medal of Freedom.

In "Is the New Morality Destroying America?" Luce attacks the moral corruptions of a sexually permissive culture, themes sounded throughout her multifaceted career. Tough, outspoken, and fiercely conservative, Luce's style of feminism balanced a respect for female independence with an affinity for traditional gender roles and morality. The American conservative movement has had several leading female lights, but few more rhetorically savvy than Clare Boothe Luce.

Delivered May 28, 1978, in Honolulu, Hawaii

I was honored—as who would not be?—by the invitation to address this Golden Circle of remarkable IBM achievers. But I confess I was somewhat floored by the subject your program producer assigned to me. He asked me to hold forth for a half-hour on the condition of morality in the United States, with special reference to the differences between America's traditional moral values and the values of the so-called "New Morality." Now even a theologian or a philosopher might hesitate to tackle so vast and complex a subject in just 30 minutes. So I suggested that he let me talk instead about, well, politics, or foreign affairs, or the Press. But he insisted that your convention wanted to talk on a subject related to morals.

Well, the invitation reminded me of a story about Archbishop Sheen, who received a telegram inviting him to deliver an address to a convention on "The World, Peace, War and the Churches." He replied: "Gentlemen, I am honored to address your great convention, but I would not want my style to be cramped by so narrow a subject. However, I would be glad to accept if you will widen the subject to include 'The Sun and the Moon and the Stars.'" So I finally agreed to talk if I could widen my subject to include, "The Traditional Morality, the New Morality, and the Universal Morality."

There's another trouble about talking about morals. It's a terribly serious subject. And a serious talk is just one step away from being a dull, not to say a soporific one. So I won't be offended if, before I finish, some of you leave. But please do so quietly, so as not to disturb those who may be sleeping.

The theme of this convention is "Involvement." Now there is one thing in which all Americans, including every one of us here, are already deeply involved. Every day of our lives, every hour of our waking days, we are all inescapably involved in making America either a more moral or a more immoral country.

So this morning, let's take a look at the direction in which we Americans are going. But first, we must begin by asking, "What are morals?"

Morals, the dictionary tells us, are a set of principles of right action and behavior for the individual. The "traditional morality" of any given society is the set of moral principles to which the great majority of its members have subscribed over a good length of time. It is the consensus which any given society has reached on what right action and decent behavior are for everybody. It is the way that society expects a person to behave, even when the law—the civil law—does not require him (or her) to do so.

One example will have to suffice. There is no law that requires a person to speak the truth, unless he is under oath to do so in a court proceeding. A person can, with legal impunity, be an habitual liar. The traditional morality of our society, however, takes a dim view of the habitual liar. Accordingly, society punishes him in the only way it can—by social ostracism.

The person who believes in the traditional principles of his society, and who also succeeds in regulating his conduct by them, is recognized by society as a "moral person." But the person who believes in these principles—who knows the difference between "right and wrong" personal conduct, but who nevertheless habitually chooses to do what he himself believes to be wrong—is looked upon by his society as an "immoral person."

But what about the person who does not believe in the traditional moral principles of his society, and who openly challenges them on grounds that he believes to be rational? Is such a person to be considered a moral or an immoral person?

Today there are many Americans who sincerely believe that many of our traditional moral values are "obsolete." They hold that some of them go against the laws of human nature, that others are no longer relevant to the economic and political condition of our society, that this or that so-called "traditional moral value" contravenes the individual's

Constitutional freedoms and legitimate pursuit of happiness. Others believe that while a moral value system is necessary as a general guideline for societal behavior, it cannot, and should not, apply to everybody. Every person is unique; no two persons are ever in exactly the same situation or "moral bind"; circumstances alter moral cases. These persons believe, in other words, that all morals are "relative," and all ethics are "situational." They argue that what is wrong behavior for others is right behavior for me, because my circumstances are different. The new principles of right action and behavior which such persons have been advancing and practicing today have come to be called "the New Morality."

But before we undertake to discuss the differences between the traditional American morality and the so-called New Morality, let us ask a most important question: Is there any such thing as a universal morality? Is there any set of moral principles which apply to everybody—everybody who has ever been born, and which has been accepted by the majority of mankind in all places and in all ages?

There is, indeed, a universal morality. It knows no race, no geographical boundaries, no time, and no particular religion. As John Ruskin, the English social reformer, wrote, "There are many religions, but there is only one morality." Immanuel Kant, the greatest of German philosophers, called it the Moral Law, which he said, governs all mankind. Kant compared this Moral Law to the Sublime Law that rules the movement of the stars and the planets. "We are doomed to be moral and cannot help ourselves," said Dr. John Haynes Holmes, the Protestant theologian.

When we study the history of human thought, we discover a truly remarkable thing—all the great minds of the world have agreed on the marks of the moral person. In all civilizations, in all ages, they have hailed truthfulness as a mark of morality. "The aim of the superior man," said Confucius, "is Truth." Plato, the Greek philosopher, held that "Truth is the beginning of every good thing both in Heaven and on earth, and he who would be blessed and happy should be from the first a partaker of truth, for then he can be trusted." "Veracity," said Thomas Huxley, the English scientist, "is the heart of morality." In Judeo-Christian lore, the Devil's other name is "The Liar."

Another mark of the moral person is honesty. "An honest man is the noblest work of God," wrote Pope in his Essay on Man. "Every honest man will suppose honest acts to flow from honest principles," said Thomas Jefferson.

The moral person is just. "Justice is the firm and continuous desire to render to everyone that which is his due," wrote Justinian. Disraeli called Justice "Truth in action." The moral person is honorable. At whatever cost to himself—including, sometimes, his very life—he does his duty by his family, his job, his country. "To an honest man," wrote Plautus, the great Roman poet, "it is an honor to have minded his duty." Two thousand years later, Woodrow Wilson voiced the same conviction. "There is no question, what the Roll of Honor in America is." Wilson said: "The Roll of Honor consists of the names of men who have squared their conduct by ideals of duty."

If, in an hour of weakness, the moral man does a thing he knows to be wrong, he confesses it, and he "takes his punishment like a soldier." And, if he harms another, even inadvertently, he tries to make restitution. He takes responsibility for his own actions. And if they turn out badly for him, he does not put the blame on others. He does not, for example, yield to the post-Freudian moral cop-out of blaming his follies and failures, his weaknesses and vices, on the way his parents treated him in childhood. Here I cannot resist mentioning the case of Tom Hansen, of Boulder, Colorado, a 24-year-old youth who is living on welfare relief funds. He is presently suing his parents for 350,000 dollars damages because, he claims, they are to blame for lousing up his life, and turning him into a failure. Adam was, of course, the first man to try to shift responsibility for his behavior onto someone else. As there was no Jewish mom to blame, he laid it on to his wife Eve.

"Absolute morality," wrote the English philosopher, Herbert Spencer, "is the regulation of conduct in such a way that pain will not be inflicted." The moral person is kind to the weak and compassionate with those who suffer.

Above all, he is courageous. Courage is the ladder on which all the other virtues mount. Plautus, a true nobleman of antiquity, wrote, "Courage stands before everything. It is what preserves our liberty, our lives, our homes, and our parents, our children, and our country. A man with courage has every blessing."

There is also one moral precept that is common to all the great religions of history. It is called the Golden Rule: "Do unto others as you would have them do to you." When Confucius was asked what he considered the single most important rule for right conduct, he replied, "Reciprocity."

The "universal morality" is based on these virtues: truthfulness, honesty, duty, responsibility, unselfishness, loyalty, honor, compassion, and courage. As Americans, we can say proudly that the traditional moral values of our society have been a reflection, however imperfect, of this universal morality. All of our great men, all of our heroes, have been exemplars of some, if not all, of these virtues.

To be sure, different cultures and civilizations have placed more emphasis on some of these virtues than on others. For example, the morality of the early Romans heavily stressed courage, honor, and duty. Even today we still call these the manly virtues, and we tend to associate them with another value we call "patriotism." In contrast, the morality of the Judeo-Christian cultures of the West have placed their heaviest emphasis on altruism, kindness, and compassion. "Though I speak with the tongue of men and angels, and have not charity," St. Paul wrote, "I am become as sounding brass or a tinkling symbol." Americans, whose traditional morality reflects the Christian virtues of compassion, donated thirty billion dollars last year to charity. Americans also tend to consider compassion for the underprivileged a greater virtue in politicians than either honor or courage.

Now, if all these virtues do indeed represent the universal morality, than what do their opposites represent? Well, lying, dishonesty, dereliction of duty, irresponsibility, dishonorable conduct, disloyalty, selfishness, cowardice, cruelty, and hypocrisy represent, of course, the universal immorality.

In passing, hypocrisy, which has been called "the compliment that vice pays to virtue," has been viewed as the height of immorality in all civilizations. "Of all villainy," cried Cicero, "there is none more base than that of the hypocrite, who at the moment he is most false, takes care to appear most virtuous." The English philosopher Henry Hazlitt called hypocrisy "the only vice that cannot be forgiven." Jesus cursed only one category of sinner, saying, "Oh woe to Ye, scribes and hypocrites!" Even the cynic and agnostic Voltaire, cried: "How inexpressible is the meanness of being a hypocrite!"

So now we are ready to ask: In what direction can we say that Americans are going? Are we, as a people, going on the high road of the universal morality or on the low road of the universal immorality?

The question is a crucial one for the future of our country. All history bears witness to the fact that there can be no public virtue without private morality. There cannot be good government except in a good society. And there cannot be a good society unless the majority of individuals in it are at least trying to be good people. This is especially true in a democracy, where leaders and representatives are chosen from the people, by the people. The character of a democratic government will never be better than the character of the people it governs. A nation that is traveling the low road is a nation that is self-destructing. It is doomed, sooner or later, to collapse from within, or to be destroyed from without. And not all its wealth, science, and technology will be able to save it. On the contrary, a decadent society will use, or rather, misuse and abuse, these very advantages in such a way as to hasten its own destruction.

Let us than face up to some of the signs which suggest that America may be traveling the low road to its own destruction.

Campus surveys show that one-third of our college students say they would cheat if they were sure they would not be caught. Forty-five percent say that they do not think that it is necessary to lead a moral life in order to be happy or successful. Sociologists note the extraordinary increase in blue and white-collar dishonesty, such as sharp business practices, dishonest advertising, juggled books and accounts, concealment of profits, and the taking and giving of bribes. These are all practices which rip-off the buying public.

Unethical practices in the professions are becoming common. Honorable members of the Bar are today appalled at the increase of shysterism in the practice of law. A recent Congressional investigation of medical practices turned up the horrifying fact that American doctors, greedy for Medicare fees, are annually performing thousands of unnecessary operations. They are dishonoring their Hippocratic oath by inflicting unnecessary pain on helpless and trusting patients for profit. The public's increasing awareness of the lack of professional integrity in many lawyers and doctors is certainly what encouraged President Carter to make his recent attacks on these two professions.

According to the polls, the majority of our citizens think that politics—and yes, post-Watergate politics—are riddled with graft, kickbacks, pay-offs, bribes, and under-the-table deals. Polls also show that our people think that most politicians have no compunction about lying their heads off in order to get elected. A great number of Americans also question the accuracy and objectivity—in short, the integrity—of journalists. They think that far too many politicians and journalists are hypocrites—quick to expose the "immorality" of those who do not hold their own political views, but quicker by far to cover up the wrong-doing of those whose views they favor.

Addressing Harvard University's graduating class in June, Aleksandr Solzhenitsyn said: "A decline in courage may be the most striking feature an outsider notices in the West . . . such a decline in courage is particularly notable among the ruling groups and the intellectual elite, causing an impression of the loss of courage by the entire society . . . Should one point out that from most ancient times a decline in courage has been considered the beginning of the end?"

A recent TV documentary about the morale of our volunteer army and our armed forces in Germany was a shocker. It revealed that one-third of our enlistees quit after a few months, finding service in the best-paid army on earth too hard on their heads or feet. One-third of our troops in Germany freely admit that they would beat it out of the forces as fast as they could the moment they thought a war was coming, and that a majority of them felt that they could not trust their comrades in battle. The officer who did the commentary on this documentary said, "What we're getting is an army of losers." The Pentagon has recently told the Congress that quotas for the armed services cannot be filled unless more women are taken in, including into the combat forces. So much for the condition of the manly virtues of duty, honor, courage in America's volunteer army.

Now I am sure that we would all agree that a rise in the crime rate indicates a weakening of society's social fiber. The staggering increase in the crime rate, especially in the rate of violent—and often utterly senseless—crime among American youth is surely a significant sign of moral decay. An even more significant sign is the impotence of our courts to cope with the enormous volume of crimes being committed. For example, of the 100,000 felony arrests made in New York City each year 97,000 or more cases are either dismissed, diverted for some non-criminal disposition, or disposed of through plea-bargaining. The average criminal who is sentenced is generally back on the streets in very short order. Studies show that most defendants arrested for serious crimes—including murder—go free. A society indifferent to the pervasiveness of crime, or too weak or terrified to bring it under control, is a society in the process of moral disintegration.

There is one other phenomenon in our society which has historically made its appearance in all decaying societies: an obsession with sex.

Sex—the procreative urge—is a mighty force. Indeed, it is the mightiest force. It is the life force. But since the dawn of history, what has distinguished man from the beasts is that he has made conscious efforts to control his lustful impulses, and to regulate and direct them into social channels. There is no primitive society known to anthropologists, no civilization known to historians, which has ever willingly consented to give its members full reign—bestial reign—of their sexual impulses. Sex morals, mores, and manners have varied enormously from age to age, and culture to culture. But sexual taboos and no-nos, sex prohibitions (and consequently, of course, inhibitions) are common to all human societies.

Now the fact that mankind had instinctively sensed that there is a right and a wrong way of handling his procreative energies strongly suggests that there may be a universal sexual morality. And so there is. And when we examine it, we find that it is this very morality that has made all human progress, and what we call civilization, possible. It is the morality that protects and preserves the basic unit of society—the family. The family is the foundation on which mankind has built all his societies. Jean Jacques Rousseau called the family "the most ancient of all societies," and "the first model of political societies."

Humans, like all animals, instinctively mate. And the male instinctively protects his mate and her offspring. If this were not true, the human race would have long since perished. For in the entire animal kingdom, there is nothing more vulnerable than a pregnant human female, or a human female giving birth. The human female carries her fetus longer, and her young remain helpless longer, than the females and young of any other species. But although humans, like all animals, instinctively mate, or pair-bond, they are not instinctively sexually faithful. Both sexes are promiscuous by nature. They come together naturally, but they do not naturally stay together. Marriage is a man-made institution. We do not know—or at least I do not know—its origins. They are lost in the mists of time. Marriage probably evolved by trial and error, as the most satisfactory way of both controlling the promiscuous impulses of the sexes, and satisfying the procreative urge in an orderly, uninterrupted basis. Bernard

Shaw wittily remarked, "Marriage offers the maximum of temptation, with the maximum of opportunity." Marriage is also the enemy of man's worst enemies—loneliness and love-lessness. In any event, marriage has been the most service-able, perdurable and, on the whole, popular of all mankind's institutions.

Thousands of years ago, the poet Homer spoke in praise of marriage: "And may the Gods accomplish your desire," he sang to the unwed maidens of Greece. "A home, a husband and harmonious converse with him—the best thing in the world being a strong house held in serenity where man and wife agree."

Marriage customs have varied greatly throughout history. But what we know about the ageless custom of marriage is this: Whether a man took unto himself one wife, or like King Solomon, 1,000 wives, whether he "courted" his bride, or bought her from her father like a head of cattle, once he took a woman as his wife, society expected him to assume the primary responsibility for her welfare and the welfare of their children. The first principle of the universal sexual morality is that the husband should protect and provide for his wife and his minor offspring as long as they need him. In many cultures, the man has also been expected to assume responsibility for his illegitimate children, or bastards, and for the fatherless or motherless children of his near relatives.

The second principle of the universal sexual morality is, in the words of St. Augustine, that "They who are cared for obey—the women their husbands, the children their parents." St. Augustine adds, however, that "in the family of the just man . . . even those who rule serve those they seem to command; for they rule not from a sense of power, but from a sense of the duty they owe to others; not because they are proud of authority, but because they love mercy."

In all human undertakings, responsibility and authority go—as they must go—hand in hand. In order for a husband and father to discharge his responsibilities, it was necessary for him to have some measure of authority—let us call it the final "say-so"—over his family. The patriarchal family has been, up to now, the family pattern of all of the world's civilizations. It will remain so until the vast majority of women are completely self-supporting.

The third principle of universal sexual morality is that spouses should be faithful to one another. Certainly this principle has always been more honored in the breach than in the observance for the simple reason that the animal side of human nature is promiscuous. But the fact remains that the faithfulness of both spouses throughout time, has been considered the ideal of marital conduct.

You may search through all the great literature of the world and you will find no words extolling marital infidelities.

While it is true that the "sins of the flesh" have always been more readily forgiven to husbands than to wives, all human societies have taken a very harsh view of men who seduce—or rape—the wives or daughters of the men of their own society.

When the Trojan, Paris, ran off with Helen, wife of the Greek King Menaleus, Greece fought a seven-year war against Troy, to protest the seduction and abduction of Helen. King David's abduction and seduction of Bathsheba, the wife of Uriah, the Hittite, scandalized his court. It also caused that God-fearing monarch great agonies of repentance. In passing, King David's repentance produced some of the world's greatest poetry—perhaps, an early proof of Sigmund Freud's theory that all the creative works of man—all his art, poetry, architecture, even his proclivity for money-making, political power, and Empire building, are *au fond*, sublimations of his consciously or subconsciously repressed sexual desires.

The fourth, and most important principle of the universal sexual morality is that moral parents, in addition to supplying the physical and emotional needs of their children should educate them to become moral adults.

"Train up the child in the way he should go; and when he is old he will not depart from it," says the Bible. John Stuart Mill wrote, "The moral training of mankind will never be adapted to the conditions of life for which all other human progress is a preparation, until they practice in the family the same moral rule which is adapted to the moral constitution of human society." In the universal family morality, parents who neglect, abuse, or desert their young or who fail to train them to become moral citizens are bad parents.

There are several other aspects of the universal sexual morality which should be mentioned. Although incest is natural among all the lower animals, and has correspondingly also made its appearance in all human societies, none has ever considered incest moral. Even in most primitive societies incest is viewed with horror. The 3,000 year old story of Oedipus Rex is the tragic story of the "guilt complex" of a man who slept—albeit accidentally—with his own mother.

History does tell us, however, that sodomy, homosexuality, and Lesbianism—virtually unknown in the lower orders—have been widely practiced, though seldom condoned, in all civilizations. But history also tells us that wherever incest, perversion, or martial unfaithfulness have become rampant, and whenever sex becomes, as we would say today, "value-free," the family structure is invariably weakened; crimes of all sorts increase, especially among the neglected young; and then more or less rapidly all other social institutions begin to disintegrate, until finally the State itself collapses. Rome is perhaps the most famous example.

In the time of Christ, when Imperial Rome was at the very height of its wealth and power, when the brick structures of the old Roman Republic had all come to be faced with gleaming marble, Rome had become a city obsessed with the pursuit of sensual pleasures. The Emperor Augustus Caesar, seeing the breakdown of the Roman family that was consequently taking place, tried to shore up the institution of marriage by passing laws making divorce more difficult and increasing punishments for adulterers, rapists, and abortionists. It was already too late. Those monsters of inequity, perversion, and violence, Caligula and Nero were already in the wings, impatiently waiting to succeed him, and to hasten the decline and fall of the Empire.

So now let us come to "sex" in America. There is no doubt that what most Americans mean when they speak of "the new morality" is the "new" sexual morality which holds that "anything goes" between consenting adults in private—and that almost anything also goes in public. The English critic, Malcolm Muggeridge had America much in mind when he wrote, "Sex is the ersatz, or substitute religion of the 20th century."

The social results of this new American ersatz religion are best seen in statistics most of which you can find in your Almanac. Today 50 percent of all marriages end in divorce, separation, or desertion. The average length of a marriage is seven years. The marriage rate and the birthrate are falling. The numbers of one-parent families and one-child families is rising. More and more young people are living together without the benefit of marriage. Many view the benefit as dubious. Premarital and extramarital sex no longer raises parental or conjugal eyebrows. The practice of "swinging," or group sex, which the ancients called "orgies," has come even to middle-class suburbia.

Despite the availability of contraceptives, there has been an enormous increase in illegitimate births, especially among 13 to 15 year-olds. Half of the children born last year in Washington, the nation's capitol, were illegitimate. The incidence of venereal diseases is increasing. Since the Supreme Court decision made abortion on demand legal, women have killed more than six million of their unborn, unwanted children. The rate of reported incest, child-molestation, rape, and child and wife abuse, is steadily mounting. (Many more of these sex connected acts of violence, while known to the police, are never brought into court, because the victims are certain that their perpetrators will not be convicted.) Run-away children, teen-age prostitution, youthful drug-addiction, and alcoholism have become great, ugly, new phenomena.

The relief rolls are groaning with women who have been divorced or deserted, together with their children. The mental-homes and rest-homes are crowded with destitute or unwanted old mothers. These two facts alone seem to suggest that American men are becoming less responsible, less moral, and certainly less manly.

Homosexuality and lesbianism are increasingly accepted as natural and alternative "lifestyles." *MS*, the official Women's Lib publication, has proclaimed that "until all women are Lesbians, there will be no true political revolution." By the same token, of course, until all men are homosexuals, the revolution will be only half a revolution. In passing, the success of the lesbian-gay revolution would end all revolutions—by ending the birth of children.

But the most obscene American phenomenon of all is the growth of commercialized sex and hard- and soft-core pornography. In the last decade, hardcore film and print porn, which features perversion, sadism, and masochism, has become a billion dollar business. It is a business which is not only tolerated, but defended by the press in the sacred name of "freedom of the press." One would find it easier to believe in this noble reason for defending the filth that is flooding the nation if the newspapers did not reap such handsome profits from advertising and reviewing porn. In my view, newspaper publishers who carry X-rated ads are no better than pimps for the porn merchants. Billy Graham may have been exaggerating when he said "America has a greater obsession with sex than Rome ever had." But he was not exaggerating very much.

Now when we examine the "new" sexual morality, what do we discover? We discover that the new sexual morality comes perilously close to being the old universal sexual immorality, whose appearance has again and again portended the decline and fall of past civilizations. Jane Addams once said, "The essence of immorality is the tendency to make an exception of myself." The principle on which the new sexual morality is based is sexual selfishness, self-indulgence, and self-gratification. Its credo is I-I-I, Me-Me-Me, and to hell with what others call sex morals.

In the 1976 Presidential campaign—for the first time in American history—the moral condition of the American family became a political issue. Candidate Jimmy Carter gave the problem particular stress.

"I find people deeply concerned about the loss . . . of moral values in our lives," he said. And like Augustus Caesar, 2,000 years before him, he fingered the cause quite correctly: "The root of this problem is the steady erosion and weakening of our families," he said. "The breakdown of the family has reached dangerous proportions." Candidate Carter also saw the relation between good government and weakened families. "If we want less government, we must have stronger families, for government steps in by necessity when families have failed. . . . It is clear that the national government should have a strong pro-family policy, but the fact is that our government has no family policy, and that is the same thing as an anti-family policy."

It is far too late in the day to review the curious ideas Mr. Carter put forth in 1976 for the steps the Federal Government might take to strengthen the American family, except to say that they largely consisted in programs for more rather than less government assumption of marital and parental responsibilities. In any event, very little has since come of Carter's promise "to construct an administration that will reverse the trends we have seen toward the breakdown of the family in our country." The truth is that very little can be done by government to shore up the family, although a great deal can be done and has been done to hasten its collapse.

But the real cause of the breakdown is the abandonment, by millions of people, beginning with husbands, wives, and parents of their interior devotion to the principles of the universal morality. To ask what can be done to reverse the trend is to ask, what can the individual members of society do? The answer is—everything.

When Goethe, the great German poet, lay on his deathbed, an old friend asked him what farewell message he had to give to the world. Goethe replied, "Let every man keep his own household clean and soon the whole world will be clean."

If not every American, but just every other American man and woman were to begin today to keep their own households clean, this process of moral decay would immediately be halted.

It is certainly not too late to hope that this will happen. There are still millions of good people in America who try, try, try to remain faithful to the American version of the universal morality, and who also bring up their children to remain faithful. These Americans constitute the true "Golden Circle" of our country. If they will try to strengthen and enlarge that circle, by only so much as one virtuous act a day, a strong and happy America will make it safely into the 21st century.

Notes

1. Albin Krebs, "Clare Boothe Luce Dies at 84: Playwright, Politician, Envoy," *New York Times,* October 10, 1987.
2. Ibid.

Ronald Reagan

"The First Inaugural"

JANUARY 20, 1981

Putting Americans Back to Work

WHEN RONALD REAGAN went to the podium on the western steps of the U.S. Capitol Building to deliver his first inaugural address, it was a cold January in Washington, DC. It was also a time of considerable concern about America's economic future and standing in the world. The annual inflation rate was in double digits as were interest rates on new home mortgages. The unemployment rate was stubbornly high and consumer confidence was low. The United States was beset by a variety of economic problems, including high gasoline prices, growing trade disputes with allied countries such as Japan, a mounting federal deficit, and the near failure of corporate titans like Chrysler.

Although Reagan would become best known for his rhetorical statements about the Cold War and the Soviet Union, in this his first speech as the president of the United States Reagan devotes almost the entire speech to these pressing domestic problems. During the 1980 presidential campaign Reagan pushed the idea that the problem did not rest with American workers, who he considered as creative and productive as they could possibly be, but with the federal government and political leaders who were encumbering workers and businesses with excessive regulation and taxation.

In this inaugural, Reagan speaks to both continuity and change. Continuity in the sense that the ordinary transfer of power from one leader to another was a hallmark of the American political tradition. At the same time, Reagan points to the necessity of reform and his enduring faith in the goodness and virtue of ordinary Americans. He outlines his free market philosophy in a single sentence: "the government is not the solution to our problem; government is the problem." Reagan also points to the mounting federal deficit, a problem that he would fail to conquer as president.

Delivered January 20, 1981, in Washington, DC

Thank you. Thank you.

Senator Hatfield, Mr. Chief Justice, Mr. President, Vice President Bush, Vice President Mondale, Senator Baker, Speaker O'Neill, Reverend Moomaw, and my fellow citizens:

To a few of us here today this is a solemn and most momentous occasion. And, yet, in the history of our nation it is a commonplace occurrence. The orderly transfer of authority as called for in the Constitution routinely takes place as it has for almost two centuries and few of us stop to think how unique we really are. In the eyes of many in the world, this every-four-year ceremony we accept as normal is nothing less than a miracle.

Mr. President, I want our fellow citizens to know how much you did to carry on this tradition. By your gracious cooperation in the transition process you have shown a watching world that we are a united people pledged to maintaining a political system which guarantees individual liberty to a greater degree than any other. And I thank you and your people for all your help in maintaining the continuity which is the bulwark of our republic.

The business of our nation goes forward.

These United States are confronted with an economic affliction of great proportions. We suffer from the longest and one of the worst sustained inflations in our national history. It distorts our economic decisions, penalizes thrift, and crushes the struggling young and the fixed-income elderly alike. It threatens to shatter the lives of millions of our people. Idle industries have cast workers into unemployment, human misery, and personal indignity.

Those who do work are denied a fair return for their labor by a tax system which penalizes successful achievement and keeps us from maintaining full productivity. But great as our tax burden is, it has not kept pace with public spending. For decades we have piled deficit upon deficit, mortgaging our future and our children's future for the temporary convenience of the present. To continue this long trend is to guarantee tremendous social, cultural, political, and economic upheavals.

You and I, as individuals, can, by borrowing, live beyond our means, but for only a limited period of time. Why then should we think that collectively, as a nation, we are not bound by that same limitation?

We must act today in order to preserve tomorrow. And let there be no misunderstanding—we're going to begin to act beginning today. The economic ills we suffer have come upon us over several decades. They will not go away in days, weeks, or months, but they will go away. They will go away because we as Americans have the capacity now, as we have had in the past, to do whatever needs to be done to preserve this last and greatest bastion of freedom.

In this present crisis, government is not the solution to our problem; government is the problem. From time to time we've been tempted to believe that society has become too complex to be managed by self-rule, that government by an elite group is superior to government for, by, and of the people. But if no one among us is capable of governing himself, then who among us has the capacity to govern someone else?

All of us together—in and out of government—must bear the burden. The solutions we seek must be equitable with no one group singled out to pay a higher price. We hear much of special interest groups. Well our concern must be for a special interest group that has been too long neglected. It knows no sectional boundaries, or ethnic and racial divisions, and it crosses political party lines. It is made up of men and women who raise our food, patrol our streets, man our mines and factories, teach our children, keep our homes, and heal us when we're sick—professionals, industrialists, shopkeepers, clerks, cabbies, and truck drivers. They are, in short, "We the People." This breed called Americans.

Well, this Administration's objective will be a healthy, vigorous, growing economy that provides equal opportunities for all Americans with no barriers born of bigotry or discrimination. Putting America back to work means putting all Americans back to work. Ending inflation means freeing all Americans from the terror of runaway living costs.

All must share in the productive work of this "new beginning," and all must share in the bounty of a revived economy.

With the idealism and fair play which are the core of our system and our strength, we can have a strong and prosperous America at peace with itself and the world. So as we begin, let us take inventory.

We are a nation that has a government—not the other way around. And this makes us special among the nations of the earth. Our Government has no power except that granted it by the people. It is time to check and reverse the growth of government which shows signs of having grown beyond the consent of the governed.

It is my intention to curb the size and influence of the Federal establishment and to demand recognition of the distinction between the powers granted to the Federal Government and those reserved to the states or to the people.

All of us—all of us need to be reminded that the Federal Government did not create the states; the states created the Federal Government.

Now, so there will be no misunderstanding, it's not my intention to do away with government. It is rather to make it work—work with us, not over us; to stand by our side, not ride on our back. Government can and must provide opportunity, not smother it; foster productivity, not stifle it. If we look to the answer as to why for so many years we achieved so much, prospered as no other people on earth, it was because here in this land we unleashed the energy and individual genius of man to a greater extent than has ever been done before.

Freedom and the dignity of the individual have been more available and assured here than in any other place on earth. The price for this freedom at times has been high, but we have never been unwilling to pay that price.

It is no coincidence that our present troubles parallel and are proportionate to the intervention and intrusion in our lives that result from unnecessary and excessive growth of Government.

It is time for us to realize that we are too great a nation to limit ourselves to small dreams. We're not, as some would have us believe, doomed to an inevitable decline. I do not believe in a fate that will fall on us no matter what we do. I do believe in a fate that will fall on us if we do nothing.

So with all the creative energy at our command, let us begin an era of national renewal. Let us renew our determination, our courage, and our strength. And let us renew our faith and our hope. We have every right to dream heroic dreams.

Those who say that we're in a time when there are no heroes—they just don't know where to look. You can see heroes every day going in and out of factory gates. Others, a handful in number, produce enough food to feed all of us and then the world beyond. You meet heroes across a counter—and they're on both sides of that counter. There are entrepreneurs with faith in themselves and faith in an idea who create new jobs, new wealth, and opportunity.

There are individuals and families whose taxes support the Government and whose voluntary gifts support church, charity, culture, art, and education. Their patriotism is quiet but deep. Their values sustain our national life.

Now I have used the words "they" and "their" in speaking of these heroes. I could say "you" and "your" because I'm addressing the heroes of whom I speak—you, the citizens of this blessed land. Your dreams, your hopes, your goals are going to be the dreams, the hopes, and the goals of this Administration, so help me God.

"The First Inaugural"

We shall reflect the compassion that is so much a part of your make-up. How can we love our country and not love our countrymen—and loving them reach out a hand when they fall, heal them when they're sick, and provide opportunity to make them self-sufficient so they will be equal in fact and not just in theory? Can we solve the problems confronting us? Well the answer is an unequivocal and emphatic "Yes." To paraphrase Winston Churchill, I did not take the oath I've just taken with the intention of presiding over the dissolution of the world's strongest economy.

In the days ahead, I will propose removing the roadblocks that have slowed our economy and reduced productivity. Steps will be taken aimed at restoring the balance between the various levels of government. Progress may be slow—measured in inches and feet, not miles—but we will progress. It is time to reawaken this industrial giant, to get government back within its means, and to lighten our punitive tax burden. And these will be our first priorities, and on these principles there will be no compromise.

On the eve of our struggle for independence a man who might've been one of the greatest among the Founding Fathers, Dr. Joseph Warren, president of the Massachusetts Congress, said to his fellow Americans,

"Our country is in danger, but not to be despaired of. On you depend the fortunes of America. You are to decide the important question upon which rest the happiness and the liberty of millions yet unborn. Act worthy of yourselves."

Well I believe we, the Americans of today, are ready to act worthy of ourselves, ready to do what must be done to ensure happiness and liberty for ourselves, our children, and our children's children. And as we renew ourselves here in our own land, we will be seen as having greater strength throughout the world. We will again be the exemplar of freedom and a beacon of hope for those who do not now have freedom.

To those neighbors and allies who share our freedom, we will strengthen our historic ties and assure them of our support and firm commitment. We will match loyalty with loyalty. We will strive for mutually beneficial relations. We will not use our friendship to impose on their sovereignty, for our own sovereignty is not for sale.

As for the enemies of freedom, those who are potential adversaries, they will be reminded that peace is the highest aspiration of the American people. We will negotiate for it, sacrifice for it; we will not surrender for it—now or ever. Our forbearance should never be misunderstood. Our reluctance for conflict should not be misjudged as a failure of will. When action is required to preserve our national security, we will act. We will maintain sufficient strength to prevail if need be, knowing that if we do so, we have the best chance of never having to use that strength.

Above all we must realize that no arsenal or no weapon in the arsenals of the world is so formidable as the will and moral courage of free men and women. It is a weapon our adversaries in today's world do not have. It is a weapon that we as Americans do have. Let that be understood by those who practice terrorism and prey upon their neighbors.

I am—I'm told that tens of thousands of prayer meetings are being held on this day; and for that I am deeply grateful. We are a nation under God, and I believe God intended for us to be free. It would be fitting and good, I think, if on each inaugural day in future years it should be declared a day of prayer.

This is the first time in our history that this ceremony has been held, as you've been told, on this West Front of the Capitol.

Standing here, one faces a magnificent vista, opening up on this city's special beauty and history. At the end of this open mall are those shrines to the giants on whose shoulders we stand. Directly in front of me, the monument to a monumental man. George Washington, father of our country. A man of humility who came to greatness reluctantly. He led America out of revolutionary victory into infant nationhood. Off to one side, the stately memorial to Thomas Jefferson. The Declaration of Independence flames with his eloquence. And then beyond the Reflecting Pool, the dignified columns of the Lincoln Memorial. Whoever would understand in his heart the meaning of America will find it in the life of Abraham Lincoln.

Beyond those moments—those monuments to heroism is the Potomac River, and on the far shore the sloping hills of Arlington National Cemetery, with its row upon row of simple white markers bearing crosses or Stars of David. They add up to only a tiny fraction of the price that has been paid for our freedom.

Each one of those markers is a monument to the kind of hero I spoke of earlier. Their lives ended in places called Belleau Wood, the Argonne, Omaha Beach, Salerno, and halfway around the world on Guadalcanal, Tarawa, Pork Chop Hill, the Chosin Reservoir, and in a hundred rice paddies and jungles of a place called Vietnam.

Under one such a marker lies a young man, Martin Treptow, who left his job in a small town barber shop in 1917 to go to France with the famed Rainbow Division. There, on the Western front, he was killed trying to carry a message between battalions under heavy fire. We're told that on his body was found a diary. On the flyleaf under the heading, "My Pledge," he had written these words:

"America must win this war. Therefore, I will work; I will save; I will sacrifice; I will endure; I will fight cheerfully and do my utmost, as if the issue of the whole struggle depended on me alone."

The crisis we are facing today does not require of us the kind of sacrifice that Martin Treptow and so many thousands of others were called upon to make. It does require, however, our best effort, and our willingness to believe in ourselves and to believe in our capacity to perform great deeds; to believe that together with God's help we can and will resolve the problems which now confront us.

And after all, why shouldn't we believe that? We are Americans.

God bless you and thank you. Thank you very much.

Ronald Reagan

"Evil Empire"

MARCH 8, 1983

Address to the National Association

of Evangelicals

RONALD REAGAN TOOK THE OATH of office for the presidency in January 1981, a time many would consider the high-water mark of the Cold War. Soviet forces had invaded Afghanistan, prompting Reagan's predecessor, Jimmy Carter, to boycott grain sales and cancel American participation in the summer Olympics held in Moscow. Poland was in turmoil as a small union called Solidarity was vying for recognition in that communist country. The Sandinistas had come to power in Nicaragua with the support of Cuba, and a civil war was raging in El Salvador and Guatemala. Hundreds of thousands of antinuclear protestors were taking to the streets of Western Europe in opposition to NATO plans to deploy Pershing II and cruise missiles.

A hallmark of Reagan's 1980 campaign for the presidency had been his commitment to pushing back Soviet power. Claiming that Jimmy Carter had weakened America and was at risk of losing Central America to communism and Western Europe to neutralism, Reagan was proposing a ramped up defense budget and an ideological offensive against Soviet communism.

The speech below is one of the most important in the context of that ideological offensive against communism. The so-called Evil Empire speech was delivered to an association of clergy. At the time there was widespread debate in the West about issues of war and peace, particularly concerning whether arms control or a policy of "peace through strength" offered the best course for preserving the peace. Reagan was beginning to launch his Strategic Defense Initiative (popularly known as Star Wars), a plan to construct a missile defense shield to reduce American vulnerability to Soviet ballistic missiles. The U.S. Catholic Bishops had come out in favor of a nuclear freeze, a position that Reagan opposed.

In this speech, Reagan lays the foundation for what he considers the moral necessities of resisting communism and totalitarianism. In so doing he made the case for a renewed religious commitment to important social issues of interest, including abortion. Moreover, Reagan's use of quotes from the likes of C. S. Lewis and Whittaker Chambers offers us a window into Reagan's beliefs on issues such as the relationship between God and Man, the nature of evil, and the importance of political courage.

The "Evil Empire" speech received widespread attention in the United States and was condemned by his political opponents as well as many in the press who objected to the president's hard-line stance toward Moscow. But Reagan's address received considerable attention inside the Soviet Union as well. Indeed, Natan Sharansky, a Soviet political prisoner at the time, recalled years later that when he heard what Reagan had said, it encouraged both him and his fellow dissidents to continue resisting the Soviet state.

Delivered March 8, 1983, in Orlando, Florida

Reverend, Clergy, all, Senator Hawkins, distinguished members of the Florida congressional delegation, and all of you: I can't tell you how you have warmed my heart with your welcome. I'm delighted to be here today.

Those of you in the National Association of Evangelicals are known for your spiritual and humanitarian work. And I would be especially remiss if I didn't discharge right now one personal debt of gratitude. Thank you for your prayers. Nancy and I have felt their presence many times in many ways. And believe me, for us they've made all the difference.

The other day in the East Room of the White House at a meeting there, someone asked me whether I was aware of all the people out there who were praying for the President. And I had to say, "Yes, I am. I've felt it. I believe in intercessionary prayer." But I couldn't help but say to that questioner after he'd asked the question that—or at least say to them that if sometimes when he was praying he got a busy signal, it was just me in there ahead of him. I think I understand how Abraham Lincoln felt when he said, "I have been driven many times to my knees by the overwhelming conviction that I had nowhere else to go." From the joy and the good feeling of this conference, I go to a political reception. Now, I don't know why, but that bit of scheduling reminds me of a story which I'll share with you.

An evangelical minister and a politician arrived at Heaven's gate one day together. And St. Peter, after doing all the necessary formalities, took them in hand to show them where their quarters would be. And he took them to a small, single room with a bed, a chair, and a table and said this was for the clergyman. And the politician was a little worried about what might be in store for him. And he couldn't believe it then when St. Peter stopped in front of a beautiful mansion with lovely grounds, many servants, and told him that these would be his quarters.

And he couldn't help but ask, he said, "But wait, how—there's something wrong—how do I get this mansion while that good and holy man only gets a single room?" And St. Peter said, "You have to understand how things are up here. We've got thousands and thousands of clergy. You're the first politician who ever made it."

But I don't want to contribute to a stereotype. So I tell you there are a great many God-fearing, dedicated, noble men and women in public life, present company included. And yes, we need your help to keep us ever-mindful of the ideas and the principles that brought us into the public arena in the first place. The basis of those ideals and principles is a commitment to freedom and personal liberty that itself is grounded in the much deeper realization that freedom prospers only where the blessings of God are avidly sought and humbly accepted.

The American experiment in democracy rests on this insight. Its discovery was the great triumph of our Founding Fathers, voiced by William Penn when he said: "If we will not be governed by God, we must be governed by tyrants." Explaining the inalienable rights of men, Jefferson said, "The God who gave us life, gave us liberty at the same time." And it was George Washington who said that "of all the dispositions and habits which lead to political prosperity, religion and morality are indispensable supports."

And finally, that shrewdest of all observers of American democracy, Alexis de Tocqueville, put it eloquently after he had gone on a search for the secret of America's greatness and genius—and he said: "Not until I went into the churches of America and heard her pulpits aflame with righteousness did I understand the greatness and the genius of America. America is good. And if America ever ceases to be good, America will cease to be great."

Well, I'm pleased to be here today with you who are keeping America great by keeping her good. Only through your work and prayers and those of millions of others can we hope to survive this perilous century and keep alive this experiment in liberty, this last, best hope of man.

I want you to know that this administration is motivated by a political philosophy that sees the greatness of America in you, her people, and in your families, churches, neighborhoods, communities: the institutions that foster and nourish values like concern for others and respect for the rule of law under God.

Now, I don't have to tell you that this puts us in opposition to, or at least out of step with, a prevailing attitude of many who have turned to a modern-day secularism, discarding the tried and time-tested values upon which our very civilization is based. No matter how well intentioned, their value system is radically different from that of most Americans. And while they proclaim that they're freeing us from superstitions of the past, they've taken upon themselves the job of superintending us by government rule and regulation. Sometimes their voices are louder than ours, but they are not yet a majority.

An example of that vocal superiority is evident in a controversy now going on in Washington. And since I'm involved I've been waiting to hear from the parents of young America. How far are they willing to go in giving to government their prerogatives as parents?

Let me state the case as briefly and simply as I can. An organization of citizens, sincerely motivated, deeply concerned about the increase in illegitimate births and abortions involving girls well below the age of consent, some time ago established a nationwide network of clinics to offer help to these girls and, hopefully, alleviate this situation. Now, again, let me say, I do not fault their intent. However, in their well-intentioned effort, these clinics decided to provide advice and birth control drugs and devices to underage girls without the knowledge of their parents.

For some years now, the federal government has helped with funds to subsidize these clinics. In providing for this, the Congress decreed that every effort would be made to maximize parental participation. Nevertheless, the drugs and devices are prescribed without getting parental consent or giving notification after they've done so. Girls termed "sexually active"—and that has replaced the word "promiscuous"—are given this help in order to prevent illegitimate birth or abortion.

Well, we have ordered clinics receiving federal funds to notify the parents such help has been given. One of the nation's leading newspapers has created the term "squeal rule" in editorializing against us for doing this, and we're being criticized for violating the privacy of young people. A judge has recently granted an injunction against an enforcement of our rule. I've watched TV panel shows discuss this issue, seen columnists pontificating on our error, but no one seems to mention morality as playing a part in the subject of sex.

Is all of Judeo-Christian tradition wrong? Are we to believe that something so sacred can be looked upon as a purely physical thing with no potential for emotional and psychological harm? And isn't it the parents' right to give counsel and advice to keep their children from making mistakes that may affect their entire lives?

Many of us in government would like to know what parents think about this intrusion in their family by government. We're going to fight in the courts. The right of parents and the rights of family take precedence over those of Washington-based bureaucrats and social engineers.

But the fight against parental notification is really only one example of many attempts to water down traditional values and even abrogate the original terms of American democracy. Freedom prospers when religion is vibrant and the rule of law under God is acknowledged. When our Founding Fathers passed the First Amendment, they sought to protect churches from government interference. They never intended to construct a wall of hostility between government and the concept of religious belief itself.

The evidence of this permeates our history and our government. The Declaration of Independence mentions the Supreme Being no less than four times. "In God We Trust" is engraved on our coinage. The Supreme Court opens its proceedings with a religious invocation. And the members of Congress open their sessions with a prayer. I just happen to believe the schoolchildren of the United States are entitled to the same privileges as Supreme Court justices and congressmen.

Last year, I sent the Congress a constitutional amendment to restore prayer to public schools. Already this session, there's growing bipartisan support for the amendment, and I am calling on the Congress to act speedily to pass it and to let our children pray.

Perhaps some of you read recently about the Lubbock school case, where a judge actually ruled that it was unconstitutional for a school district to give equal treatment to religious and nonreligious student groups, even when the group meetings were being held during the students' own time. The First Amendment never intended to require government to discriminate against religious speech.

Senators Denton and Hatfield have proposed legislation in the Congress on the whole question of prohibiting discrimination against religious forms of student speech. Such legislation could go far to restore freedom of religious speech for public school students. And I hope the Congress considers these bills quickly. And with your help, I think it's possible we could also get the constitutional amendment through the Congress this year.

More than a decade ago, a Supreme Court decision literally wiped off the books of fifty states' statutes protecting the rights of unborn children. Abortion on demand now takes the lives of up to one and a half million unborn children a year. Human life legislation ending this tragedy will someday pass the Congress, and you and I must never rest until it does. Unless and until it can be proven that the unborn child is not a living entity, then its right to life, liberty, and the pursuit of happiness must be protected.

You may remember that when abortion on demand began, many, and indeed, I'm sure many of you, warned that the practice would lead to a decline in respect for human life, that the philosophical premises used to justify abortion on demand would ultimately be used to justify other attacks on the sacredness of human life—infanticide or mercy killing. Tragically enough, those warnings proved all too true. Only last year a court permitted the death by starvation of a handicapped infant.

I have directed the Health and Human Services Department to make clear to every health care facility in the United States that the Rehabilitation Act of 1973 protects all handicapped persons against discrimination based on handicaps, including infants. And we have taken the further step of requiring that each and every recipient of federal funds who provides health care services to infants must post and keep posted in a conspicuous place a notice stating that "discriminatory failure to feed and care for handicapped infants in this facility is prohibited by federal law." It also lists a twenty-four-hour, toll-free number so that nurses and others may report violations in time to save the infant's life.

In addition, recent legislation introduced by—in the Congress by Representative Henry Hyde of Illinois not only increases restrictions on publicly financed abortions; it also addresses this whole problem of infanticide. I urge the Congress to begin hearings and to adopt legislation that will protect the right of life to all children, including the disabled or handicapped.

Now, I'm sure that you must get discouraged at times, but there you've done better than you know, perhaps. There's a great spiritual awakening in America, a renewal of the traditional values that have been the bedrock of America's goodness and greatness.

One recent survey by a Washington-based research council concluded that Americans were far more religious than the people of other nations; 95 percent of those surveyed expressed a belief in God and a huge majority believed the Ten Commandments had real meaning in their lives. And another study has found that an overwhelming majority of Americans disapprove of adultery, teenage sex, pornography, abortion, and hard drugs. And this same study showed a deep reverence for the importance of family ties and religious belief.

I think the items that we've discussed here today must be a key part of the nation's political agenda. For the first time the Congress is openly and seriously debating and dealing with the prayer and abortion issues and that's enormous progress right there. I repeat: America is in the midst of a spiritual awakening and a moral renewal. And with your biblical keynote, I say today, "Yes, let justice roll on like a river, righteousness like a never-failing stream."

Now, obviously, much of this new political and social consensus I've talked about is based on a positive view of American history, one that takes pride in our country's accomplishments and record. But we must never forget that no government schemes are going to perfect man. We know that living in this world means dealing with what philosophers would call the phenomenology of evil or, as theologians would put it, the doctrine of sin.

There is sin and evil in the world, and we're enjoined by Scripture and the Lord Jesus to oppose it with all our might. Our nation, too, has a legacy of evil with which it must deal. The glory of this land has been its capacity for transcending the moral evils of our past. For example, the long struggle of minority citizens for equal rights, once a source of disunity and civil war is now a point of pride for all Americans. We must never go back. There is no room for racism, anti-Semitism, or other forms of ethnic and racial hatred in this country.

I know that you've been horrified, as have I, by the resurgence of some hate groups preaching bigotry and prejudice. Use the mighty voice of your pulpits and the powerful standing of your churches to denounce and isolate these hate groups in our midst. The commandment given us is clear and simple: "Thou shalt love thy neighbor as thyself."

But whatever sad episodes exist in our past, any objective observer must hold a positive view of American history, a history that has been the story of hopes fulfilled and dreams made into reality. Especially in this century, America has kept alight the torch of freedom, but not just for ourselves but for millions of others around the world.

And this brings me to my final point today. During my first press conference as president, in answer to a direct question, I pointed out that, as good Marxist-Leninists, the Soviet leaders have openly and publicly declared that the only morality they recognize is that which will further their cause, which is world revolution. I think I should point out I was only quoting Lenin, their guiding spirit, who said in 1920 that they repudiate all morality that proceeds from supernatural ideas—that's their name for religion—or ideas that are outside class conceptions. Morality is entirely subordinate to the interests of class war. And everything is moral that is necessary for the annihilation of the old, exploiting social order and for uniting the proletariat.

Well, I think the refusal of many influential people to accept this elementary fact of Soviet doctrine illustrates a historical reluctance to see totalitarian powers for what they are. We saw this phenomenon in the 1930s. We see it too often today.

This doesn't mean we should isolate ourselves and refuse to seek an understanding with them. I intend to do everything I can to persuade them of our peaceful intent, to remind them that it was the West that refused to use its nuclear monopoly in the forties and fifties for territorial gain and which now proposes a 50 percent cut in strategic ballistic missiles and the elimination of an entire class of land-based, intermediate-range nuclear missiles.

At the same time, however, they must be made to understand we will never compromise our principles and standards. We will never give away our freedom. We will never abandon our belief in God. And we will never stop searching for a genuine peace. But we can assure none of these things America stands for through the so-called nuclear freeze solutions proposed by some.

The truth is that a freeze now would be a very dangerous fraud, for that is merely the illusion of peace. The reality is that we must find peace through strength.

I would agree to a freeze if only we could freeze the Soviets' global desires. A freeze at current levels of weapons would remove any incentive for the Soviets to negotiate seriously in Geneva and virtually end our chances to achieve the major arms reductions which we have proposed. Instead, they would achieve their objectives through the freeze.

A freeze would reward the Soviet Union for its enormous and unparalleled military buildup. It would prevent the essential and long overdue modernization of United States and allied defenses and would leave our aging forces increasingly vulnerable. And an honest freeze would require extensive prior negotiations on the systems and numbers to be limited and on the measures to ensure effective verification and compliance. And the kind of a freeze that has been suggested would be virtually impossible to verify. Such a major effort would divert us completely from our current negotiations on achieving substantial reductions.

A number of years ago, I heard a young father, a very prominent young man in the entertainment world, addressing a tremendous gathering in California. It was during the time of the Cold War, and communism and our own way of life were very much on people's minds. And he was speaking to that subject. And suddenly, though, I heard him saying, "I love my little girls more than anything." And I said to myself, "Oh, no, don't. You can't—don't say that." But I had underestimated him. He went on: "I would rather see my little girls die now, still believing in God, than have them grow up under communism and one day die no longer believing in God."

There were thousands of young people in that audience. They came to their feet with shouts of joy. They had instantly recognized the profound truth in what he had said, with regard to the physical and the soul and what was truly important.

Yes, let us pray for the salvation of all of those who live in that totalitarian darkness. Pray they will discover the joy of knowing God. But until they do, let us be aware that while they preach the supremacy of the State, declare its omnipotence over individual man, and predict its eventual domination of all peoples on the earth, they are the focus of evil in the modern world.

It was C. S. Lewis who, in his unforgettable *Screwtape Letters*, wrote: "The greatest evil is not done now in those sordid 'dens of crime' that Dickens loved to paint. It is not even done in concentration camps and labor camps. In those we see its final result. But it is conceived and ordered; moved, seconded, carried and minuted in clear, carpeted, warmed, and well-lighted offices, by quiet men with white collars and cut fingernails and smooth-shaven cheeks who do not need to raise their voice."

Well, because these quiet men do not raise their voices, because they sometimes speak in soothing tones of brotherhood and peace, because, like other dictators before them, they're always making "their final territorial demand," some would have us accept them at their word and accommodate ourselves to their aggressive impulses. But if history teaches anything, it teaches that simpleminded appeasement or wishful thinking about our adversaries is folly. It means the betrayal of our past, the squandering of our freedom.

So, I urge you to speak out against those who would place the United States in a position of military and moral inferiority. You know, I've always believed that old Screwtape reserved his best efforts for those of you in the Church. So, in your discussions of the nuclear freeze proposals, I urge you to beware the temptation of pride—the temptation of blithely declaring yourselves above it all and label both sides equally at fault, to ignore the facts of history and the aggressive impulses of an evil empire, to simply call the arms race a giant misunderstanding and thereby remove yourself from the struggle between right and wrong and good and evil.

I ask you to resist the attempts of those who would have you withhold your support for our efforts, this administration's efforts, to keep America strong and free, while we negotiate real and verifiable reductions in the world's nuclear arsenals and one day, with God's help, their total elimination.

While America's military strength is important, let me add here that I've always maintained that the struggle now going on for the world will never be decided by bombs or rockets, by armies or military might. The real crisis we face today is a spiritual one; at root, it is a test of moral will and faith.

Whittaker Chambers, the man whose own religious conversion made him a witness to one of the terrible traumas of our time, the Hiss–Chambers case, wrote that the crisis of the Western world exists to the degree in which the West is indifferent to God, the degree to which it collaborates in communism's attempt to make man stand alone without God. And then he said, for Marxism–Leninism is actually the second-oldest faith, first proclaimed in the Garden of Eden with the words of temptation, "Ye shall be as gods."

The Western world can answer this challenge, he wrote, "but only provided that its faith in God and the freedom He enjoins is as great as communism's faith in Man."

I believe we shall rise to the challenge. I believe that communism is another sad, bizarre chapter in human history whose last—last pages even now are being written. I believe this because the source of our strength in the quest for human freedom is not material, but spiritual. And because it knows no limitation, it must terrify and ultimately triumph over those who would enslave their fellow man. For in the words of Isaiah: "He giveth power to the faint; and to them that have no might He increased strength. But they that wait upon the Lord shall renew their strength; they shall mount up with wings as eagles; they shall run, and not be weary."

Yes, change your world. One of our Founding Fathers, Thomas Paine, said, "We have it within our power to begin the world over again." We can do it, doing together what no one church could do by itself.

God bless you and thank you very much.

Phyllis Schlafly

"Child Abuse in the Classroom"

JUNE 26, 1987

Conference of the Legal Services of the New York City Board of Education

MODERN FEMINISM'S HISTORY cannot be retold without serious consideration of its most fearless nemesis—Phyllis Schlafly.
Named one of the one hundred most important women of the
twentieth century by the *Ladies' Home Journal*, Schlafly's centrality to the American conservative movement is hard to overstate.
Indeed, her 1964 best-selling book, *A Choice Not an Echo*, sold 3
million copies and is often cited as having contributed significantly to the nomination of Barry Goldwater for president.

Born in 1924 in St. Louis, Missouri, Phyllis Schlafly would
later put herself through college by working the night shift at the
St. Louis Ordnance Plant where she tested ammunition by firing
rifles and machine guns. After graduating with a BA from Washington University in St. Louis, Schlafly then went on to receive her
master's in government from Harvard University. In 1978, a full
thirty-three years after receiving her degree from Harvard, she
would receive her JD from Washington University Law School.

Over the span of her impressive career, Schlafly has authored
or edited twenty books on a diverse range of topics. Still, her opposition to the radical feminist movement remains her signature
achievement, the result of her epic decade-long battle against and
victory over passage of the Equal Rights Amendment (ERA) to the

United States Constitution, an effort that seemed, at the time, an almost foregone conclusion. The Senate had passed the measure 84 to 8. Likewise, the measure had sailed through the House 354 to 23. From there, ERA went to the states, thirty of which approved it during the first year of ratification. To achieve passage, only eight more states were needed.[1]

Enter profamily activist Phyllis Schlafly. After engaging in hundreds of debates, writing for national publications, and speaking out in state capitals around the country against an amendment that she argued would rob women of many of the legal rights they possessed, including ending the female exemption from the draft, Phyllis Schlafly and her organization, Eagle Forum, had effectively killed the ERA.

Her defeat of the ERA, however, was just one of the many causes she has taken up over her long public career. But if there is one common denominator among her many efforts on behalf of the American conservative movement, it remains her commitment to the preservation of the traditional family.

In the speech that follows, Schlafly addresses the New York School Board and speaks out against the infusion of secular humanism in the textbooks and curriculum materials used by public schools across the country. Drawing on her background as a lawyer, as well as her experience as a former member of the Commission on the Bicentennial of the U.S. Constitution, she argues that the razing of traditional values and morality operative in many public school textbooks "is a direct attack on the First Amendment rights of those who believe that God created us, and that He created a moral law that we should obey."

In addition to her legislative achievements and her creation of the Eagle Forum, now in existence for thirty-four years, Schlafly's fearless style and relentless drive has inspired a new generation of female conservatives, most notably Ann Coulter, who consider Schlafly their hero. Indeed, when Schlafly asked Coulter to write the foreword for one of her books, Coulter began, "Writing the foreword to a book by Phyllis Schlafly is like being the warm-up band for the Rolling Stones. Though conservative women in my generation are often compared to Schlafly, all of us combined could never match the titanic accomplishments of this remarkable woman. Schlafly is unquestionably one of the most important people of the twentieth century. Among her sex, she is rivaled only by Margaret Thatcher."[2]

Delivered June 26, 1987, in Pocono Manor, Pennsylvania
Thank you very much for those kind words. And good morning, ladies and gentlemen. I do thank the sponsors of this meeting for presenting such a balanced program, and I thank you for your willingness to hear another side of the issue. Perhaps this is a first. I wish that school boards had been willing to do what you're doing today for the last twenty years. But I certainly do sincerely compliment you on your willingness to listen to some thoughts that you may not agree with.

First, I think it's important to know what frame of reference I am coming from. I am not part of the religious right. I am not a fundamentalist who is trying to impose my religion on public school children. I come from a state where prayer was banned from the public schools at the time of World War I, and I am not seeking to put it back in. I am not an enemy of public schools. I had a very happy public school experience. I certainly believe in education. I come from a family where the women and men have been college graduates for more than a century. I wanted college so much that, having no money, I worked my own way through college without any aid of any type, in a grimy night-shift job, forty-eight hours a week. My husband and I have financed six children though thirty-seven years of university education at seven secular universities. So, indeed, I care about education.

I think these three lawsuits that have been mentioned today are symptomatic of two movements which are current in our society. On the one hand, we have those people who seem to believe that the public school child is a captive of the administrators of the public schools, and that the schools can do anything they want with the children pretty much as though they were guinea pigs. Those people seem to think that, if parents presume to interfere with or criticize curriculum, they are troublemakers, mischief-makers, censors, bigots, and the whole host of epithets that is spun out by the ACLU and People for the American Way.

On the other hand, there are those of us who believe that, since the children—and they are minor children in public schools—are a captive audience under compulsory school laws, the authority figure must be limited and restricted by two other elements.

First of all, we have the power and rights of the parents. Certainly, it is good constitutional law in our nation that the parents are the primary educators of their children. They have the right to safeguard the religion, the morals, the attitudes, the values, and the family privacy of their children.

Secondly, the schools are subject to the taxpayers and the citizens of our nation. I come from the frame of reference that anybody who spends the taxpayers' money simply has to put up with citizens' surveillance. Ronald Reagan has to put up with it. The Congressmen have to put up with it. The state legislators have to put up with it. And teachers, school administrators, and librarians have to put up with it. This is one of the penalties of being able to spend the taxpayers' money. Those who don't like other citizens looking over their shoulders and second-guessing their judgment should really go into some other line of work where they're not spending the taxpayers' money.

So, we find it very distressing when schools resent parents and citizens looking over their shoulders. I think it is their absolute right. Congress has the same right to look over what the President is doing. Forty years ago it was not necessary to identify these different categories or types of right because the public schools had a very high reputation in our land. I can remember forty years ago when conservative speakers who made some critical remarks about public schools were literally hooted down. Public schools enjoyed a high reputation like the Post Office. They were sacred cows. Nobody could attack them and get by with it.

That public confidence, frankly, is no longer there. And let me explain one reason why it's no longer there. Thirty-two years ago, I was ready to enter my first child in public school, thinking that the first task of the school was to teach the child to read. We now know that there are at least twenty-three million illiterates in this county, adults who have been through the public schools and didn't learn how to read.

Well, I discovered that thirty-two years ago when I entered my first child in public school and found that they didn't teach him to read. They only taught little children to memorize a few words by guessing at them from the picture on the page. That is why I kept all my six children out of school until I taught them to read at home—so that they would be good readers, and so they would not be six of the twenty-three million functional illiterates in our country today. This is not a matter of Secular Humanism or morals or affluence versus poverty or anything else.

No public school in my area taught reading. Schools only taught silly little word guessing, which was a cheat on the taxpayers and a cheat on the children. We see the results today.

Thirty-two years ago I didn't know anybody else who taught her own child. Today there are about a million who are doing that because, indeed, they feel cheated by the public schools.

In the mid-1970s something else came into the schools to use up the time that could not be spent in reading the great books and the classics, which formerly children were able to do. This new element that came into public schools was best summarized and described by Senator Sam Hayakawa, who was a university president before he became a United States Senator. He called it a "heresy" in public school education. He said that, instead of teaching children knowledge and basic skills, the purpose of education has become group therapy. That's the best way to describe what has happened in the schools.

In public school classrooms, children are required to discuss feelings and emotions and attitudes. They are confronted with all sorts of moral dilemmas, instead of being given the facts and the knowledge they need. As a result of what happened, Hayakawa was a major promoter of a federal law passed in 1978 called the Protection of Pupil Rights Amendment, which said that schools should not give psychological testing or treatment to public school children in a list of areas that includes family privacy, sexual matters, and other personal matters, without the prior written consent of their parents.

The purpose of this law was to prevent the schools from engaging in this psychological probing, invasion of privacy, or manipulation of values. What people had discovered was that so much of education has adopted the techniques best described in Sidney Simon's book on *Values Clarification*.

The education establishment was so powerful that no regulations were issued on this law until 1984. But the parents were discovering what was happening to their children, and they didn't like it. They discovered that these psychological manipulations in the classroom constituted a continuing attack on their religion, on their morals, on their family, and on parents. And, yes, we do believe that the continuing attack is so gross as to rise to the level of a violation of the First Amendment rights of parents and their children.

What happened is best illustrated by the classic lifeboat game, which is probably used in every school in this country. I had a reporter tell me that she had some variation of it at every level of elementary and secondary education. This is the game where the child is taught that ten people are in a sinking lifeboat, and the child must throw five of them out to drown. Which five will you kill? Will it be the senior citizen, or the policeman, or the pregnant woman, or the college co-ed, or the black militant, or whoever? You pick which you will kill.

This game is played so widely, in many variations—the fall-out shelter, the kidney machine, starting a new race, and so forth. To explain what's wrong about this game, we have the example of the creative child who answered the lifeboat problem by saying, "Jesus brought another boat, and nobody had to drown." That child was creative, but she got an "F" on her paper. That explains what values clarification does. Don't let anybody tell you it's neutral. It is not neutral in any shape or form. It is a direct attack on the religion and the values of those of us who believe that God created us, and that it is not up to the child to play God and decide who lives and who dies.

The curriculum is filled with these moral dilemmas. The reason we know about so many of them is that, in 1984, the Department of Education conducted hearings across the country, where parents could come and describe what had happened to their own children. Those hearings had no press, but you can read much of the testimony in my book called *Child Abuse in the Classroom*. My book is filled with the authentic testimonies of parents. They told how the children were given moral dilemmas as: Stand up in class and give a good example of when it's okay to lie; write a paper on when it's all right to steal; let's discuss which kind of drugs you will take, how much and how many.

These moral dilemmas never tell the child that anything is wrong. The child is taken through all the areas of sex, with obscene descriptions, and discussions and role-playing, and other psychological manipulations in the classroom. You can call this secular humanism, you can call it situation ethics, you can call it group therapy, you can call it psychological manipulations, you can call it counseling. You can call it no-name. But whatever it is, it is completely prevalent and widespread in the public schools, and it is a direct attack on the First Amendment rights of those who believe that God created us, and that He created a moral law that we should obey. There's nothing neutral about the way these values are taught. The option that we should abide by God's law is never offered.

I am very excited about the Alabama textbook case because it has finally brought out of the closet a situation that has been going on for fifteen, twenty years, without media coverage or public attention. I noticed that Mr. Bradford said how surprised he was, when he got into this case, to discover that home ec is about sex. Well, if you've been reading the textbooks, you would have known that for the last fifteen years. And this is why parents are so upset.

What Judge Hand's decision in the Alabama textbook case did was, simply, to give the child who believes in God the same right as the atheist. What's wrong with that?

In the Jaffree case, the Supreme Court held that little atheist Jaffree had the right to be in the public school classroom, and not be embarrassed when his peer said a prayer, or spoke about God. In the Alabama textbook case, Judge Hand's decision simply gives the child who believes in God the same right as the atheist. I do believe that the child has a right to be in the public school classroom, and not have his religion, his morals, and his family belittled or harassed, or told that they are irrelevant, or be presented with moral dilemmas which tell him that he can decide what is moral or legal.

We hear about giving the child a choice. Of course, the child, if accosted by the drug peddler, has to make a choice whether to buy or not. But it is so wrong to tell the child in class that he is capable of making a choice on an issue which the law has already decided. The law has already decided that illegal drugs are bad, and that he must not take drugs. That is what the school should teach.

Since the First Amendment seems to prohibit the school from teaching belief in God and His moral commandments, the school must not be permitted to teach that there isn't any God, that God did not create the world, and did not give us His moral commandments. It becomes a fact question to see if they're teaching that.

If you look at what was involved in these Alabama textbooks, you'll find textbooks saying that "what is right or wrong depends more on your own judgment than on what someone tells you to do." That's a direct attack on religion. One book tells the teacher to design a bulletin board showing conflicting values held by young people and their parents. This is absolute mischief-making between the child and his parents.

Another textbook teaches that a family is a group of people who live together. That's not what a family is. A family starts with a marriage between a man and a woman. We find a textbook telling a child that, "in democratic families, every member has a voice in running the family, and parents and teenagers should decide together about curfew, study time, chores, allowances, and use of the car." Where does anybody get the idea that the school can tell the child that he's got a right to decide when he uses the car?

Here's another one. "Steps in decision-making can apply to something so simple as buying a new pair of shoes. They can also be applied to more complex decisions which involve religious preferences, use of alcohol, tobacco, and drugs." Where did schools get the idea that schools can teach children that the family should be democratic and that the children should make these decisions?

Here's another textbook: "In the past, families were often like dictatorships. One person, or two, made all the decisions." Is that mischief-making? You bet it's mischief-making. Here's one that seems to say that it's okay if people want to experience parenthood without marrying.

Here's a quotation from another textbook: "People who have strong prejudices are called bigots. Bigots are devoted to their own church, party, or belief." That really puts your parents down, doesn't it!

Here's a long passage saying that divorce is an acceptable way of solving a problem. Then it calls on the class to role-play the circumstances that might lead the child to choose a divorce. The school has no right to attack the morals of children by telling them that divorce is acceptable. Whose idea is it that schools can do this?

Actually, the Alabama school textbooks are probably pretty mild compared to a lot of others we find around the rest of the country. We just succeeded in exposing one in Seattle that came right out and said that promiscuity should not be labeled good or bad, that premarital sexual intercourse is acceptable for both men and women, that morality is individual, it's what you think it is, that homosexuality is okay, that prostitution should be legalized, that it is not deviant for teenagers to watch others performing sex acts through binoculars or windows, that alternatives to

PHYLLIS SCHLAFLY

traditional marriage such as group sex and open marriage are okay, and then asks the child if he'd like to join such a group.

It took eighteen months and finally some TV cameras, to get the curriculum committee to say they would replace that textbook. And yet, it had been the textbook in a mandatory course in the Seattle public school system since 1978.

Then you come to your own video, "Sex, Drugs and AIDS," which I understand has been so controversial in New York, that it is now being revised. But the original version has now gone all over the country. It blows my mind to think that anybody could believe it is constitutional, or acceptable, to present a video in the public school classroom teaching children that fornication and sodomy are acceptable behavior so long as you use condoms, and telling them that homosexuality is all right, which is exactly what that video does. I cannot believe that anybody could approve such an evil video for use in the public school classroom. It is a direct attack on the First Amendment right of those who believe that fornication and sodomy are wrong.

What we want is the same right for people who believe in God and His commandments as the atheist has already established. Whatever you call it, this no-name ideology, it all boils down to an attack on religion, a war on parental rights, a betrayal of trust, and yes, indeed what I called it in my book, "child abuse in the classroom." What a terrible thing it is to indicate, imply, and even tell children that sexual intercourse with males or females, of the same sex or the opposite sex, is okay and socially acceptable! Yet, that is widely taught in the public schools across the country.

Because of this situation, we have prepared our Student Bill of Rights. None of these rights has been litigated, because the school administrators have a great battery of tax-paid lawyers. The parents who object to this are generally vilified, condemned, ostracized, isolated, and harassed through the media, and they have to go out and hire their own lawyers.

The general attitude of most public school administrators, when parents make objections, is: If you don't like it, take your child out and to a private school. That is not an acceptable answer. Our position is that the child who believes in God and His Commandments has a right to be in the public school classroom, and the right to be there without having his religion, his morals, and his family degraded, belittled, subjected to clarification or role-playing, or subjected to any of the psychological dilemmas that are presented by authority figures, who tell them in every way possible, overtly and indirectly, that there is no right or wrong answer, that anything the little fifth grader decides will be perfectly all right.

I am very happy about the Alabama textbook case, and the East Tennessee case, and all of the similar cases, because while the public schools with their great battery of lawyers may be able to win in the courts, and the media are clearly on their side, these cases are not increasing respect for the public schools. It is very useful that these cases have occurred. They have brought into public debate issues which should have been debated for the last twenty years. Thank you for listening.

Notes

1. Phyllis Schlafly, *Feminist Fantasies* (Dallas: Spence Publishing, 2003).
2. Ibid., xiii.

Barbara Bush

"The Controversy Ends Here"

JUNE 1, 1990

Wellesley College Commencement Address

THE MOTHER OF the 43rd president, the wife of the 41st, and the great-great grand-grand niece of the 14th, Barbara Pierce Bush, it seems, was born to be at the center of American presidential power. Yet growing up in Rye, New York, Bush's aspirations were far from regal. In fact, one might say her dreams were simple—mundane even.

Born June 8, 1925, Barbara Pierce at age twenty met World War II Navy pilot turned Yale University baseball player George Herbert Walker Bush. Pierce would later decide to forgo completion of her degree from Smith College in order to marry Bush. "Faith, family, and friends are the most important things in life," she would later say.

The Bushes had six children, one of whom, Robin, would die of leukemia at the age of four, a tragedy that Mrs. Bush says affected her and young George W. Bush deeply. More than anything, Robin's death confirmed Barbara Bush's abiding belief in the importance of family and her role in raising her own. And it was precisely this personal choice—to stay home with her children—that would come under intense attack when, instead of author Alice Walker, the women of Wellesley College would have as their commencement speaker First Lady Barbara Bush.

Rarely has a commencement speaker withstood the kind of controversy and national media scrutiny as that which befell

Barbara Bush leading up to her June 1, 1990, speech. Of Wellesley's six hundred graduating seniors, 150 had signed a petition that read in part, "Barbara Bush has gained recognition through the achievements of her husband . . . [Wellesley] teaches us that we will be rewarded on the basis of our own merit, not on that of a spouse."

Once the *New York Times* ran a front-page story on the topic, the First Lady wrote in her diary that "my phone rang off the hook" and that she even received a phone call from a supportive Richard Nixon. "I can't go anywhere that I am not asked about it," she wrote, "That darn Wellesley flap has taken on a life of its own. There are more editorials, more talk shows. . . . It's putting too much pressure on."[1]

By the day of her speech, the rhetorical bar Barbara Bush had to clear seemed insurmountable. On the one hand, she needed to ingratiate herself to a hostile live audience. But on the other hand, she had to do so in a way that legitimized her decision to choose family over a professional career. What's more, she would need to accomplish all of these objectives in front of a live nationally televised audience.

Through an artful blend of audience analysis, storytelling, humor, and personal testimony, Barbara Bush advanced a subtle if powerful thesis: by imposing narrow definitions of the "proper" roles of women—like her protestors did—genuine diversity is diminished. In this way, Bush turned liberal notions of tolerance and a woman's right to choose her own course in life on their head. Moreover, Bush did so in a way that not only disarmed her critics but also endeared them to her. As she said in her speech, "The controversy ends here. But our conversation is only beginning."

Delivered June 1, 1990, in Wellesley, Massachusetts

Thank you. Thank you, very much. Thank you very, very much, President Keohane. Mrs. Gorbachev, Trustees, Faculty, Parents, and I should say, Julia Porter, class president, and certainly my new best friend, Christine Bicknell—and, of course, the Class of 1990. I am really thrilled to be here today, and very excited, as I know you all must be, that Mrs. Gorbachev could join us.

These are exciting times. They're exciting in Washington, and I have really looked forward to coming to Wellesley. I thought it was going to be fun. I never dreamt it would be this much fun. So, thank you for that.

More than ten years ago, when I was invited here to talk about our experiences in the People's Republic of China, I was struck by both the natural beauty of your campus and the spirit of this place.

Wellesley, you see, is not just a place but an idea—an experiment in excellence in which diversity is not just tolerated, but is embraced. The essence of this spirit was captured in a moving speech about tolerance given last year by a student body president of one of your sister colleges. She related the story by Robert Fulghum about a young pastor, finding himself in charge of some very energetic children, hit upon the game called "Giants, Wizards, and Dwarfs." "You have to decide now," the pastor instructed the children, "which you are—a giant, a wizard, or a dwarf?" At that, a small girl tugging at his pants leg, asked, "But where do the mermaids stand?" And the pastor tells her there are no mermaids. And she says, "Oh yes there are. I am a mermaid."

Now this little girl knew what she was, and she was not about to give up on either her identity, or the game. She intended to take her place wherever mermaids fit into the scheme of things. Where do the mermaids stand? All of those who are different, those who do not fit the boxes and the pigeonholes? "Answer that question," wrote Fulghum, "And you can build a school, a nation, or a whole world." As that very wise young woman said, "Diversity, like anything worth having, requires effort. Effort to learn about and respect difference, to be compassionate with one another, to cherish our own identity, and to accept unconditionally the same in others."

You should all be very proud that this is the Wellesley spirit. Now I know your first choice today was Alice Walker—guess how I know!—known for *The Color Purple*.

Instead you got me—known for the color of my hair! Alice Walker's book has a special resonance here. At Wellesley, each class is known by a special color. For four years the Class of '90 has worn the color purple. Today you meet on Severance Green to say goodbye to all of that, to begin a new and very personal journey, to search for your own true colors.

In the world that awaits you, beyond the shores of Lake Waban, no one can say what your true colors will be. But this I do know: You have a first class education from a first class school. And so you need not, probably cannot, live a "paint-by-numbers" life. Decisions are not irrevocable. Choices do come back. And as you set off from Wellesley, I hope that many of you will consider making three very special choices.

The first is to believe in something larger than yourself, to get involved in some of the big ideas of our time. I chose literacy because I honestly believe that if more people could read, write, and comprehend, we would be that much closer to solving so many of the problems that plague our nation and our society.

And early on I made another choice which I hope you'll make as well. Whether you are talking about education, career, or service, you're talking about life—and life really must have joy. It's supposed to be fun!

One of the reasons I made the most important decision of my life, to marry George Bush, is because he made me laugh. It's true, sometimes we've laughed through our tears. But that shared laughter has been one of our strongest bonds. Find the joy in life, because as Ferris Bueller said on his day off, "Life moves pretty fast; and ya don't stop and look around once in a while, ya gonna miss it!"

(I am not going to tell George ya clapped more for Ferris than ya clapped for George.)

The third choice that must not be missed is to cherish your human connections: your relationships with family and friends. For several years, you've had impressed upon you the importance to your career of dedication and hard

BARBARA BUSH

work. And, of course, that's true. But as important as your obligations as a doctor, a lawyer, a business leader will be, you are a human being first. And those human connections—with spouses, with children, with friends—are the most important investments you will ever make.

At the end of your life, you will never regret not having passed one more test, winning one more verdict, or not closing one more deal. You will regret time not spent with a husband, a child, a friend, or a parent.

We are in a transitional period right now, fascinating and exhilarating times, learning to adjust to changes and the choices we, men and women, are facing. As an example, I remember what a friend said, on hearing her husband complain to his buddies that he had to babysit. Quickly setting him straight, my friend told her husband that when it's your own kids, it's not called babysitting.

Now, maybe we should adjust faster; maybe we should adjust slower. But whatever the era, whatever the times, one thing will never change: fathers and mothers, if you have children, they must come first. You must read to your children. And you must hug your children. And you must love your children. Your success as a family, our success as a society, depends not on what happens in the White House, but on what happens inside your house.

For over fifty years, it was said that the winner of Wellesley's annual hoop race would be the first to get married. Now they say, the winner will be the first to become a CEO. Both of those stereotypes show too little tolerance for those who want to know where the mermaids stand. So I want to offer a new legend: the winner of the hoop race will be the first to realize her dream—not society's dreams—her own personal dream.

And who knows? Somewhere out in this audience may even be someone who will one day follow in my footsteps, and preside over the White House as the President's spouse.

I wish him well!

Well, the controversy ends here. But our conversation is only beginning. And a worthwhile conversation it has been.

So as you leave Wellesley today, take with you deep thanks for the courtesy and the honor you have shared with Mrs. Gorbachev and with me. Thank you. God bless you. And may your future be worthy of your dreams.

Note

1. Barbara Bush, *Barbara Bush: A Memoir* (New York: Scribners, 1994), 338.

Newt Gingrich

"The Contract with America"

JANUARY 4, 1995

Acceptance Speech as Speaker of the House

NEWT GINGRICH was born in 1943 to a military family. He spent much of his youth attending schools at various military installations around the world. After graduating from Emory University he went on to obtain his MA and PhD in history from Tulane. For the next eight years he taught history at West Georgia College before being elected to the U.S. Congress in 1978. Gingrich moved through the ranks of the Republican Party on Capitol Hill, which appeared destined for the role as a permanent minority; since 1946, the Democrats had been in control of Congress. But Gingrich remained undeterred, envisioning a GOP majority. Most political observers remained skeptical, believing that demographic changes, regional political allegiances, and the constellation of interests that made up the Democratic coalition all but ensured a permanent majority.

Gingrich, however, believed he could engineer a Republican takeover not by moving to the middle, but by speaking with a clear, conservative vision. It was in many respects an echo of the Reagan message: limited government, traditional values, and a strong national defense. But to this he added a series of agenda points that he called the Contract with America. Gingrich's Contract called for greater accountability for the Congress, term limits for elected officials, limitations on the ability of Congress to raise taxes, and a commitment to empowering individuals, instead of the federal government. To the surprise of most political observers, during the 1994 midterm elections, the GOP took control of the House of Representatives for the first time in forty years. Undoubtedly the so-called Gingrich Revolution was helped along by middle-class concerns about the course the Clinton administration had charted regarding health care reform and taxes, as well as several congressional scandals. Yet in the end, Gingrich offered voters a clear package of policies and an ideological vision to embrace.

What follows is the speech Gingrich delivered to his fellow members as he was inaugurated as the Speaker of the U.S. House of Representatives. The speech is both a restatement of the Contract with America as well as an attempt to reach across party lines to begin to reform American government. While crediting the liberal wing of the Democratic Party with ending segregation, Gingrich challenged Democrats to join the new GOP majority in replacing "the welfare state with an opportunity society." In so doing the newly elected Speaker cites several influences on his thinking, including Marvin Olasky's book *The Tragedy of American Compassion*.

Much of Gingrich's vision remains central to today's Republican Party. Indeed, Gingrich's call for an opportunity society seemed to presage President George W. Bush's call for "compassionate conservatism."

Delivered January 4, 1995, in Washington, DC

Let me say first of all that I am deeply grateful to my good friend, Dick Gephardt. When my side maybe overreacted to your statement about ending 40 years of Democratic rule, I could not help but look over at Bob Michel, who has often been up here and who knows that everything Dick said was true. This is difficult and painful to lose, and on my side of the aisle, we have for 20 elections been on the losing side. Yet there is something so wonderful about the process by which a free people decides things.

In my own case, I lost two elections, and with the good help of my friend Vic Fazio came close to losing two others. I am sorry, guys, it just did not quite work out. Yet I can tell you that every time when the polls closed and I waited for the votes to come in, I felt good, because win or lose, we have been part of this process.

In a little while, I am going to ask the dean of the House, John Dingell, to swear me in, to insist on the bipartisan nature of the way in which we together work in this House. John's father was one of the great stalwarts of the New Deal, a man who, as an FDR Democrat, created modern America. I think that John and his father represent a tradition that we all have to recognize and respect, and recognize that the America we are now going to try to lead grew from that tradition and is part of that great heritage.

I also want to take just a moment to thank Speaker Foley, who was extraordinarily generous, both in his public utterances and in everything that he and Mrs. Foley did to help Marianne and me, and to help our staff make the transition. I think that he worked very hard to reestablish the dignity of the House. We can all be proud of the reputation that he takes and of the spirit with which he led the Speakership. Our best wishes go to Speaker and Mrs. Foley.

I also want to thank the various House officers, who have been just extraordinary. I want to say for the public record that faced with a result none of them wanted, in a situation I suspect none of them expected, that within 48 hours every officer of this House reacted as a patriot, worked overtime, bent over backwards, and in every way helped us. I am very grateful, and this House I think owes a debt of gratitude to every officer that the Democrats elected two years ago.

This is a historic moment. I was asked over and over, how did it feel, and the only word that comes close to adequate is overwhelming. I feel overwhelmed in every way, overwhelmed by all the Georgians who came up, overwhelmed by my extended family that is here, overwhelmed by the historic moment. I walked out and stood on the balcony just outside of the Speaker's office, looking down the Mall this morning, very early. I was just overwhelmed by the view, with two men I will introduce and know very, very well. Just the sense of being part of America, being part of this great tradition, is truly overwhelming.

I have two gavels. Actually, Dick happened to use one. Maybe this was appropriate. This was a Georgia gavel I just got this morning, done by Dorsey Newman of Tallapoosa. He decided that the gavels he saw on TV weren't big enough or strong enough, so he cut down a walnut tree in his backyard, made a gavel, put a commemorative item on it, and sent it up here.

So this is a genuine Georgia gavel, and I am the first Georgia Speaker in over 100 years. The last one, by the way, had a weird accent, too. Speaker Crisp was born in Britain. His parents were actors and they came to the United States—a good word, by the way, for the value we get from immigration.

Second, this is the gavel that Speaker Martin used. I am not sure what it says about the inflation of Government, to put them side by side, but this was the gavel used by the last Republican Speaker.

I want to comment for a minute on two men who served as my leaders, from whom I learned so much and who are here today. When I arrived as a freshman, the Republican Party, deeply dispirited by Watergate and by the loss of the Presidency, banded together and worked with a leader who helped pave the way for our great party victory of 1980, a man who just did a marvelous job. I cannot speak too highly of what I learned about integrity and leadership and courage from serving with him in my freshman term. He is here with us again today. I hope all of you will recognize Congressman John Rhodes of Arizona.

I want to say also that at our request, the second person was not sure he should be here at all, then he thought he was going to hide in the back of the room. I insisted that he come on down front, someone whom I regard as a mentor. I think virtually every Democrat in the House would say he is a man who genuinely cares about, loves the House, and represents the best spirit of the House. He is a man who I studied under and, on whom I hope as Speaker I can always rely for advice.

I hope frankly I can emulate his commitment to this institution and his willingness to try to reach beyond his personal interest and partisanship. I hope all of you will join me in thanking for his years of service, Congressman Bob Michel of Illinois.

I am very fortunate today. My Mom and my Dad are here, they are right up there in the gallery. Bob and Kit Gingrich. I am so delighted that they were both able to be here. Sometimes when you get to my age, you cannot have everyone near you that you would like to have. I cannot say how much I learned from my Dad and his years of serving in the U.S. Army and how much I learned from my Mother, who is clearly my most enthusiastic cheerleader.

My daughters are here up in the gallery, too. They are Kathy Love and her husband Paul, and Jackie and her husband Mark Zyler. Of course, the person who clearly is my closest friend and my best adviser and whom if I listened to about 20 percent more, I would get in less trouble, my wife Marianne, is in the gallery as well.

I have a very large extended family between Marianne and me. They are virtually all in town, and we have done our part for the Washington tourist season. But I could not help, when I first came on the floor earlier, I saw a number of the young people who are here. I met a number of the children who are on the floor and the young adults, who are close to 12 years of age. I could not help but think that sitting in the back rail near the center of the House is one of my nephews, Kevin McPherson, who is 5. My nieces Susan Brown, who is 6, and Emily Brown, who is 8, and Laura McPherson, who is 9, are all back there, too. That is probably more than I was allowed to bring on, but they are my nieces and my nephews. I have two other nephews a little older who are sitting in the gallery.

I could not help but think as a way I wanted to start the Speakership and to talk to every Member, that in a sense these young people around us are what this institution is really all about. Much more than the negative advertising and the interest groups and all the different things that make politics all too often cynical, nasty, and sometimes frankly just plain miserable, what makes politics worthwhile is the choice, as Dick Gephardt said, between what we see so tragically on the evening news and the way we try to work very hard to make this system of free, representative self-government work. The ultimate reason for doing that is these children, the country they will inherit, and the world they will live in.

We are starting the 104th Congress. I do not know if you have every thought about this, but for 208 years, we bring together the most diverse country in the history of the world. We send all sorts of people here. Each of us could find at least one Member we thought was weird. I will tell you, if you went around the room the person chosen to be weird would be different for virtually every one of us. Because we do allow and insist upon the right of a free people to send an extraordinary diversity of people here.

Brian Lamb of C-SPAN read to me Friday a phrase from de Tocqueville that was so central to the House. I have been reading Remini's biography of Henry Clay, as the first strong Speaker, always preferred the House. He preferred the House to the Senate although he served in both. He said the House is more vital, more active, more dynamic, and more common.

This is what de Tocqueville wrote: "Often there is not a distinguished man in the whole number. Its members are almost all obscure individuals whose names bring no associations to mind. They are mostly village lawyers, men in trade, or even persons belonging to the lower classes of society."

If we include women, I do not know that we would change much. But the word "vulgar" in de Tocqueville's time had a very particular meaning. It is a meaning the world would do well to study in this room. You see, de Tocqueville was an aristocrat. He lived in a world of kings and princes. The folks who come here do so by the one single act that their citizens freely chose them. I do not care what your ethnic background is, or your ideology. I do not care if you are younger or older. I do not care if you are born in America or if you are a naturalized citizen. Every one of the 435 people has equal standing because their citizens freely sent them. Their voice should be heard and they should have a right to participate. It is the most marvelous act of a complex giant country trying to argue and talk. And, as Dick Gephardt said, to have a great debate, to reach great decisions, not through a civil war, not by bombing one of our regional capitals, not by killing a half million people, and not by having snipers. Let me say unequivocally, I condemn all acts of violence against the law by all people for all reasons. This is a society of law and a society of civil behavior.

Here we are as commoners together, to some extent Democrats and Republicans, to some extent liberals and conservatives, but Americans all. Steve Gunderson today gave me a copy of *The Portable Abraham Lincoln*. He suggested there is much for me to learn about our party, but I would also say that it does not hurt to have a copy of the portable FDR.

This is a great country of great people. If there is any one factor or acts of my life that strikes me as I stand up here as the first Republican in 40 years to do so. When I first became whip in 1989, Russia was beginning to change, the Soviet Union as it was then. Into my whip's office one day came eight Russians and a Lithuanian, members of the Communist Party, newspaper editors. They asked me, "What does a whip do?"

They said, "In Russia we have never had a free parliament since 1917 and that was only for a few months, so what do you do?"

I tried to explain, as Dave Bonior or Tom DeLay might now. It is a little strange if you are from a dictatorship to explain you are called the whip but you do not really have a whip, you are elected by the people you are supposed to pressure—other members. If you pressure them too much they will not reelect you. On the other hand, if you do not pressure them enough they will not reelect you. Democracy is hard. It is frustrating.

So our group came into the Chamber. The Lithuanian was a man in his late sixties, and I allowed him to come up here and sit and be Speaker, something many of us have done with constituents. Remember, this is the very beginning of perestroika and glasnost. When he came out of the chair, he was physically trembling. He was almost in tears. He said, "Ever since World War II, I have remembered what the Americans did and I have never believed the propaganda. But I have to tell you, I did not think in my life that I would be able to sit at the center of freedom."

It was one of the most overwhelming, compelling moments of my life. It struck me that something I could not help but think of when we were here with President Mandela. I went over and saw Ron Dellums and thought of the great work Ron had done to extend freedom across the planet. You get that sense of emotion when you see something so totally different than you had expected. Here was a man who reminded me first of all that while presidents are important, they are in effect an elected kingship, that this and the other body across the way are where freedom has to be fought out. That is the tradition I hope that we will take with us as we go to work.

Today we had a bipartisan prayer service. Frank Wolf made some very important points. He said, "We have to recognize that many of our most painful problems as a country are moral problems, problems of dealing with ourselves and with life."

He said character is the key to leadership and we have to deal with that. He preached a little bit. I do not think he thought he was preaching, but he was. It was about a spirit of reconciliation. He talked about caring about our spouses and our children and our families. If we are not prepared to model our own family life beyond just having them here for one day, if we are not prepared to care about our children and we are not prepared to care about our families, then by what arrogance do we think we will transcend our behavior to care about others? That is why with Congressman Gephardt's help we have established a bipartisan task force on the family. We have established the principle that we are going to set schedules we stick to so families can count on time to be together, built around school schedules so that families can get to know each other, and not just by seeing us on C-SPAN.

I will also say that means one of the strongest recommendations of the bipartisan committee, is that we have 17 minutes to vote. This is the bipartisan committee's recommendation, not just mine. They pointed out that if we take the time we spent in the last Congress where we waited for one more Member, and one more, and one more, that we literally can shorten the business and get people home if we will be strict and firm. At one point this year we had a 45-minute vote. I hope all of my colleagues are paying attention because we are in fact going to work very hard to have 17-minute votes and it is over. So, leave on the first bell, not the second bell. Okay? This may seem particularly inappropriate to say on the first day because this will be the busiest day on opening day in congressional history.

I want to read just a part of the Contract with America. I don't mean this as a partisan act, but rather to remind all of us what we are about to go through and why. Those of us who ended up in the majority stood on these steps and signed a contract, and here is part of what it says:

On the first day of the 104th Congress the new Republican majority will immediately pass the following reforms aimed at restoring the faith and trust of the American people in their government: First, require all laws that apply to the rest of the country also to apply equally to the Congress. Second, select a major, independent auditing firm to conduct a comprehensive audit of the Congress for waste, fraud, or abuse. Third, cut the number of House committees and cut committee staffs by a third. Fourth, limit the terms of all committee chairs. Fifth, ban the casting of proxy votes in committees. Sixth, require committee meetings to be open to the public. Seven, require a three-fifths majority vote to pass a tax increase. Eight, guarantee an honest accounting of our federal budget by implementing zero baseline budgeting.

Now, I told Dick Gephardt last night that if I had to do

it over again we would have pledged within 3 days that we will do these things, but that is not what we said. So we have ourselves in a little bit of a box here.

Then we go a step further. I carry the *TV Guide* version of the contract with me at all times.

We then say that within the first 100 days of the 104th Congress we shall bring to the House floor the following bills, each to be given full and open debate, each to be given a full and clear vote, and each to be immediately available for inspection. We made it available that day. We listed 10 items. A balanced budget amendment and line-item veto, a bill to stop violent criminals, emphasizing among other things an effective and enforceable death penalty. Third was welfare reform. Fourth, legislation protecting our kids. Fifth was to provide tax cuts for families. Sixth was a bill to strengthen our national defense. Seventh was a bill to raise the senior citizens' earning limit. Eighth was legislation rolling back Government regulations. Ninth was a common-sense legal reform bill, and tenth was congressional term limits legislation.

Our commitment on our side, and this is an absolute obligation, is first of all to work today until we are done. I know that is going to inconvenience people who have families and supporters. But we were hired to do a job, and we have to start today to prove we will do it. Second, I would say to our friends in the Democratic Party that we are going to work with you, and we are really laying out a schedule working with the minority leader to make sure that we can set dates certain to go home. That does mean that if two or three weeks out we are running short we will, frankly, have longer sessions on Tuesday, Wednesday, and Thursday. We will try to work this out on a bipartisan basis to, in a workmanlike way, get it done. It is going to mean the busiest early months since 1933.

Beyond the Contract I think there are two giant challenges. I know I am a partisan figure. But I really hope today that I can speak for a minute to my friends in the Democratic Party as well as my own colleagues, and speak to the country about these two challenges so that I hope we can have a real dialog. One challenge is to achieve a balanced budget by 2002. I think both Democratic and Republican Governors will say we can do that but it is hard. I do not think we can do it in a year or two. I do not think we ought to lie to the American people. This is a huge, complicated job.

The second challenge is to find a way to truly replace the current welfare state with an opportunity society.

Let me talk very briefly about both challenges. First, on the balanced budget I think we can get it done. I think the baby boomers are now old enough that we can have an honest dialog about priorities, about resources, about what works, and what does not work. Let me say I have already told Vice President Gore that we are going to invite him to address a Republican conference. We would have invited him in December but he had to go to Moscow, I believe there are grounds for us to talk together and to work together, to have hearings together, and to have task forces together. If we set priorities, if we apply the principles of Edwards Deming, and of Peter Drucker we can build on the Vice President's reinventing government effort and we can focus on transforming, not just cutting. The choice becomes not just do you want more or do you want less, but are there ways to do it better? Can we learn from the private sector, can we learn from Ford, IBM, from Microsoft, from what General Motors has had to go through? I think on a bipartisan basis we owe it to our children and grandchildren to get this Government in order and to be able to actually pay our way. I think 2002 is a reasonable time frame. I would hope that together we could open a dialog with the American people.

I have said that I think Social Security ought to be off limits, at least for the first 4 to 6 years of the process, because I think it will just destroy us if we try to bring it into the game. But let me say about everything else, whether it is Medicare, or it is agricultural subsidies, or it is defense or anything that I think the greatest Democratic President of the 20th century, and in my judgment the greatest President of the 20th century, said it right. On March 4, 1933, he stood in braces as a man who had polio at a time when nobody who had that kind of disability could be anything in public life. He was President of the United States, and he stood in front of this Capitol on a rainy March day and he said, "We have nothing to fear but fear itself." I want every one of us to reach out in that spirit and pledge to live up to that spirit, and I think frankly on a bipartisan basis. I would say to Members of the Black and Hispanic Caucuses that I would hope we could arrange by late spring to genuinely share districts. You could have a Republican who frankly may not know a thing about your district agree to come for a long weekend with you, and you will agree to go for a long weekend with them. We begin a dialog and an openness that is totally different than people are used to seeing in politics in America. I believe if we do that we can then create a dialog that can lead to a balanced budget.

But I think we have a greater challenge. I do want to pick up directly on what Dick Gephardt said, because he said it right. No Republican here should kid themselves about it. The greatest leaders in fighting for an integrated America in the 20th century were in the Democratic Party. The fact is, it was the liberal wing of the Democratic Party that ended segregation. The fact is that it was Franklin Delano Roosevelt who gave hope to a Nation that was in distress and could have slid into dictatorship. Every Republican has much to learn from studying what the Democrats did right.

But I would say to my friends in the Democratic Party that there is much to what Ronald Reagan was trying to get done. There's much to what is being done today by Republicans like Bill Weld, and John Engler, and Tommy Thompson, and George Allen, and Christy Whitman, and Pete Wilson. There is much we can share with each other.

We must replace the welfare state with an opportunity society. The balanced budget is the right thing to do. But it does not in my mind have the moral urgency of coming to grips with what is happening to the poorest Americans.

I commend to all Marvin Olasky's *The Tragedy of American Compassion*. Olasky goes back for 300 years and looks at what has worked in America, how we have helped people rise beyond poverty, and how we have reached out to save people. He may not have the answers, but he has the right sense of where we have to go as Americans.

I do not believe that there is a single American who can see a news report of a 4-year-old thrown off of a public housing project in Chicago by other children and killed and not feel that a part of your heart went, too. I think of my nephew in the back, Kevin, and how all of us feel about our children. How can any American read about an 11-year-old buried with his teddy bear because he killed a 14-year-old, and then another 14-year-old killed him, and not have some sense of "My God, where has this country gone?" How can we not decide that this is a moral crisis equal to segregation, equal to slavery? How can we not insist that every day we take steps to do something?

I have seldom been more shaken than I was after the election when I had breakfast with two members of the Black Caucus. One of them said to me, "Can you imagine what it is like to visit a first-grade class and realize that every fourth or fifth young boy in that class may be dead or in jail within 15 years? And they are your constituents and you are helpless to change it?" For some reason, I do not know why, maybe because I visit a lot of schools, that got through. I mean, that personalized it. That made it real, not just statistics, but real people.

Then I tried to explain part of my thoughts by talking about the need for alternatives to the bureaucracy, and we got into what I think frankly has been a pretty distorted and cheap debate over orphanages.

Let me say, first of all, my father, who is here today, was a foster child. He was adopted as a teenager. I am adopted. We have relatives who were adopted. We are not talking out of some vague impersonal Dickens "Bleak House" middle-class intellectual model. We have lived the alternatives.

I believe when we are told that children are so lost in the city bureaucracies that there are children who end up in dumpsters, when we are told that there are children doomed to go to schools where 70 or 80 percent of them will not graduate, when we are told of public housing projects that are so dangerous that if any private sector ran them they would be put in jail, and the only solution we are given is, "Well, we will study it, we will get around to it," my only point is that this is unacceptable. We can find ways immediately to do things better, to reach out, break through the bureaucracy and give every young American child a better chance.

Let me suggest to you Morris Schectman's new book. I do not agree with all of it, but it is fascinating. It is entitled *Working without a Net*. It is an effort to argue that in the 21st century we have to create our own safety nets. He draws a distinction between caring and caretaking. It is worth every American reading.

He said caretaking is when you bother me a little bit, and I do enough, I feel better because I think I took care of you. That is not any good to you at all. You may be in fact an alcoholic and I just gave you the money to buy the bottle that kills you, but I feel better and go home. He said caring is actually stopping and dealing with the human being, trying to understand enough about them to genuinely make sure you improve their life, even if you have to start with a conversation like, "If you will quit drinking, I will help you get a job." This is a lot harder conversation than, "I feel better. I gave him a buck or 5 bucks."

I want to commend every Member on both sides to look carefully. I say to those Republicans who believe in total privatization, you cannot believe in the Good Samaritan and explain that as long as business is making money we can walk by a fellow American who is hurt and not do something. I would say to my friends on the left who believe there has never been a government program that was not worth keeping, you cannot look at some of the results we now have and not want to reach out to the humans and forget the bureaucracies.

If we could build that attitude on both sides of this aisle, we would be an amazingly different place, and the country would begin to be a different place.

We have to create a partnership. We have to reach out to the American people. We are going to do a lot of important things. Thanks to the House Information System and Congressman Vern Ehlers, as of today we are going to be online for the whole country, every amendment, every conference report. We are working with C-SPAN and others, and Congressman Gephardt has agreed to help on a bipartisan basis to make the building more open to television, more accessible to the American people. We have talk radio hosts here today for the first time. I hope to have a bipartisan effort to make the place accessible for all talk radio hosts of all backgrounds, no matter their ideology. The House Historian's office is going to be more aggressively run on a bipartisan basis to reach out to Close Up, and to other groups to teach what the legislative struggle is about. I think over time we can and will this spring rethink campaign reform and lobbying reform and review all ethics, including the gift rule.

But that isn't enough. Our challenge shouldn't be just to balance the budget or to pass the Contract. Our challenge should not be anything that is just legislative. We are supposed to, each one of us, be leaders. I think our challenge has to be to set as our goal, and maybe we are not going to get there in 2 years. This ought to be the goal that we go home and we tell people we believe in: that there will be a Monday morning when for the entire weekend not a single child was killed anywhere in America; that there will be a Monday morning when every child in the country went to a school that they and their parents thought prepared them as citizens and prepared them to compete in the world market; that there will be a Monday morning where it was easy to find a job or create a job, and your own Government did not punish you if you tried.

We should not be happy just with the language of politicians and the language of legislation. We should insist that our success for America is felt in the neighborhoods, in the communities, is felt by real people living real lives who can say, "Yes, we are safer, we are healthier, we are better educated, America succeeds."

This morning's closing hymn at the prayer service was the "Battle Hymn of the Republic." It is hard to be in this building, look down past Grant to the Lincoln Memorial and not realize how painful and how difficult that battle hymn is. The key phrase is, "As he died to make men holy, let us live to make men free."

It is not just political freedom, although I agree with everything Congressman Gephardt said earlier. If you cannot afford to leave the public housing project, you are not free. If you do not know how to find a job and do not know how to create a job, you are not free. If you cannot find a place that will educate you, you are not free. If you are afraid to walk to the store because you could get killed, you are not free.

So as all of us over the coming months sing that song, "As he died to make men holy, let us live to make men free." I want us to dedicate ourselves to reach out in a genuinely nonpartisan way to be honest with each other. I promise each of you that without regard to party my door is going to be open. I will listen to each of you. I will try to work with each of you. I will put in long hours, and I will guarantee that I will listen to you first. I will let you get it all out before I give you my version, because you have been patient with me today, and you have given me a chance to set the stage.

But I want to close by reminding all of us of how much bigger this is than us. Because beyond talking with the American people, beyond working together, I think we can only be successful if we start with our limits. I was very struck this morning with something Bill Emerson used, a very famous quote of Benjamin Franklin, at the point where the Constitutional Convention was deadlocked. People were tired, and there was a real possibility that the Convention was going to break up. Franklin, who was quite old and had been relatively quiet for the entire Convention, suddenly stood up and was angry, and he said:

"I have lived, sir, a long time, and the longer I live the more convincing proofs I see of this truth, that God governs in the affairs of men, and if a sparrow cannot fall to the ground without His notice, is it possible that an empire can rise without His aid?"

At that point the Constitutional Convention stopped. They took a day off for fasting and prayer.

Then, having stopped and come together, they went back, and they solved the great question of large and small States. They wrote the Constitution, and the United States was created. All I can do is pledge to you that, if each of us will reach out prayerfully and try to genuinely understand each other, if we will recognize that in this building we symbolize America, and that we have an obligation to talk with each other, then I think a year from now we can look on the 104th Congress as a truly amazing institution without regard to party, without regard to ideology. We can say, "Here America comes to work, and here we are preparing for those children a better future."

Thank you. Good luck and God bless you.

George W. Bush

"Our Mission and Our Moment"

SEPTEMBER 20, 2001

The War Address

George Walker Bush was born on July 6, 1946, in New Haven, Connecticut, just blocks from Yale University where he would later attend college. But it was the culture and spirit of Midland, Texas, the place where Bush grew up, that would define his values, political sensibilities, and demeanor. Taken together this blend of beliefs would fall under the banner phrase for which he is known: "compassionate conservatism."

Still, while West Texas would shape Bush, his alma mater was not without its influence. During his 2001 commencement speech at Yale, for example, Bush jokingly credited the university as having been the place where he mastered the art of oratory: "I did take English here, and I took a class called 'The History and Practice of American Oratory,' taught by Rollin G. Osterweis. And, President Levin, I want to give credit where credit is due. I want the entire world to know this—everything I know about the spoken word, I learned right here at Yale."

The joke, of course, reflects the perception of Bush as an inarticulate bumbler, as someone who mangles the English language. But it also reflects another current that runs through Bush's life story. It reveals his willingness—*desire* even—to be "misunderestimated," as he once famously flubbed. From his MBA at Harvard, to his management of the Texas Rangers, to his stunning defeat of former Texas governor Ann Richards, to his unlikely defeat of former vice president Al Gore, all the way to his reelection over Senator John Kerry, George W. Bush has always found a way to exceed expectations. And on September 20, 2001, that is precisely what he did.

As noted presidential rhetoric scholar David Zarefsky has written, "On September 20, 2001, President George W. Bush rose to the occasion. He and his writers found the right words, the right themes, the right voice."[1]

Having suffered the worst attack in U.S. history, President Bush faced a rhetorical hurdle of inestimable proportions. A fearful and anxious nation had questions that demanded answers—and leadership. As veteran *Washington Post* journalists Dan Balz and Bob Woodward wrote, "No presidential speech in recent history would be more important to national morale or more scrutinized than this one." In Philadelphia, for example, an exhibition professional hockey game had to be stopped when fans demanded that the arena play Bush's address on the video screens overhead.[2]

The speech not only sought to heal a nation, it also established a new direction in American foreign policy: preemption. Some have suggested that the Bush doctrine—any country that aids or harbors a terrorist will be considered a "hostile regime"—represents a victory for neoconservatives. Yet Bush himself has never embraced that term. Instead, imbued with the religious tones often found in presidential crisis rhetoric, Bush reaffirmed his conservative worldview by drawing a clear delineation between good and evil. As the president put it, "Freedom and fear, justice and cruelty, have always been at war, and we know that God is not neutral between them."

While Bush's speech was not without its liberal critics, to date the address is widely viewed as his finest rhetorical performance. Even the president's political adversaries showered him with praise. Democratic senator Dianne Feinstein scored the speech a "ten," saying, "He put forward a battle plan, he inspired Americans, he brought us all together." Former vice presidential rival Senator Joseph Lieberman agreed, adding, "I thought the speech was stirring."

But for President Bush, it was the response of the hockey fans in Philadelphia that made the greatest impact. "When I really realized the extent to which America wanted to be led was when they stopped the hockey game in Philadelphia. It was unbelievable. . . . They wanted to hear what the commander in chief, the president of the United States, had to say during this moment."[3]

On September 20, 2001, 80 million Americans huddled around their televisions to find "Our Mission and Our Moment."

Delivered September 20, 2001, in Washington, DC

Mr. Speaker, Mr. President Pro Tempore, members of Congress, and fellow Americans:

In the normal course of events, Presidents come to this chamber to report on the state of the Union. Tonight, no such report is needed. It has already been delivered by the American people.

We have seen it in the courage of passengers, who rushed terrorists to save others on the ground—passengers like an exceptional man named Todd Beamer. And would you please help me to welcome his wife, Lisa Beamer, here tonight.

We have seen the state of our Union in the endurance of rescuers, working past exhaustion. We have seen the unfurling of flags, the lighting of candles, the giving of blood, the saying of prayers in English, Hebrew, and Arabic. We have seen the decency of a loving and giving people who have made the grief of strangers their own.

My fellow citizens, for the last nine days, the entire world has seen for itself the state of our Union—and it is strong.

Tonight we are a country awakened to danger and called to defend freedom. Our grief has turned to anger, and anger to resolution. Whether we bring our enemies to justice, or bring justice to our enemies, justice will be done.

I thank the Congress for its leadership at such an important time. All of America was touched on the evening of the tragedy to see Republicans and Democrats joined together on the steps of this Capitol, singing "God Bless America." And you did more than sing; you acted, by delivering $40 billion to rebuild our communities and meet the needs of our military.

Speaker Hastert, Minority Leader Gephardt, Majoi ity Leader Daschle, and Senator Lott, I thank you for y‹ friendship, for your leadership and for your service to ‹ country.

And on behalf of the American people, I thank the w ..u for its outpouring of support. America will never forget the sounds of our National Anthem playing at Buckingham Palace, on the streets of Paris, and at Berlin's Brandenburg Gate.

We will not forget South Korean children gathering to pray outside our embassy in Seoul, or the prayers of sympathy offered at a mosque in Cairo. We will not forget moments of silence and days of mourning in Australia and Africa and Latin America.

Nor will we forget the citizens of 80 other nations who died with our own: dozens of Pakistanis; more than 130 Israelis; more than 250 citizens of India; men and women from El Salvador, Iran, Mexico, and Japan; and hundreds of British citizens. America has no truer friend than Great Britain. Once again, we are joined together in a great cause—so honored the British Prime Minister has crossed an ocean to show his unity with America. Thank you for coming, friend.

On September the 11th, enemies of freedom committed an act of war against our country. Americans have known wars—but for the past 136 years, they have been wars on foreign soil, except for one Sunday in 1941. Americans have known the casualties of war—but not at the center of a great city on a peaceful morning. Americans have known surprise attacks—but never before on thousands of civilians. All of this was brought upon us in a single day—and night fell on a different world, a world where freedom itself is under attack.

Americans have many questions tonight. Americans are asking: Who attacked our country? The evidence we have gathered all points to a collection of loosely affiliated terrorist organizations known as al-Qaeda. They are some of the same murderers indicted for bombing American embassies in Tanzania and Kenya, and responsible for bombing the USS *Cole*.

Al-Qaeda is to terror what the mafia is to crime. But its goal is not making money; its goal is remaking the world—and imposing its radical beliefs on people everywhere.

The terrorists practice a fringe form of Islamic extremism that has been rejected by Muslim scholars and the vast majority of Muslim clerics—a fringe movement that perverts the peaceful teachings of Islam. The terrorists' directive commands them to kill Christians and Jews, to kill all Americans, and make no distinction among military and civilians, including women and children.

This group and its leader—a person named Osama bin Laden—are linked to many other organizations in different countries, including the Egyptian Islamic Jihad and the Islamic Movement of Uzbekistan. There are thousands of these terrorists in more than 60 countries. They are recruited from their own nations and neighborhoods and brought to camps in places like Afghanistan, where they are trained in the tactics of terror. They are sent back to their homes or sent to hide in countries around the world to plot evil and destruction.

The leadership of al-Qaeda has great influence in Afghanistan and supports the Taliban regime in controlling most of that country. In Afghanistan, we see al-Qaeda's vision for the world.

Afghanistan's people have been brutalized—many are starving and many have fled. Women are not allowed to attend school. You can be jailed for owning a television. Religion can be practiced only as their leaders dictate. A man can be jailed in Afghanistan if his beard is not long enough.

The United States respects the people of Afghanistan—after all, we are currently its largest source of humanitarian aid—but we condemn the Taliban regime. It is not only repressing its own people, it is threatening people everywhere by sponsoring and sheltering and supplying terrorists. By aiding and abetting murder, the Taliban regime is committing murder.

And tonight, the United States of America makes the following demands on the Taliban: Deliver to United States authorities all the leaders of al-Qaeda who hide in your land. Release all foreign nationals, including American citizens, you have unjustly imprisoned. Protect foreign journalists, diplomats, and aid workers in your country. Close immediately and permanently every terrorist training camp in Afghanistan, and hand over every terrorist, and every person in their support structure, to appropriate authorities. Give the United States full access to terrorist training camps, so we can make sure they are no longer operating.

These demands are not open to negotiation or discussion. The Taliban must act, and act immediately. They will hand over the terrorists, or they will share in their fate.

I also want to speak tonight directly to Muslims throughout the world. We respect your faith. It's practiced freely by many millions of Americans, and by millions more in countries that America counts as friends. Its teachings are good and peaceful, and those who commit evil in the name of Allah blaspheme the name of Allah. The terrorists are traitors to their own faith, trying, in effect, to hijack Islam itself. The enemy of America is not our many Muslim friends; it is not our many Arab friends. Our enemy is a radical network of terrorists, and every government that supports them.

Our war on terror begins with al-Qaeda, but it does not end there. It will not end until every terrorist group of global reach has been found, stopped and defeated.

Americans are asking, why do they hate us? They hate what we see right here in this chamber—a democratically elected government. Their leaders are self-appointed. They hate our freedoms—our freedom of religion, our freedom of speech, our freedom to vote and assemble and disagree with each other.

They want to overthrow existing governments in many Muslim countries, such as Egypt, Saudi Arabia, and Jordan. They want to drive Israel out of the Middle East. They want to drive Christians and Jews out of vast regions of Asia and Africa.

These terrorists kill not merely to end lives, but to disrupt and end a way of life. With every atrocity, they hope that

America grows fearful, retreating from the world and forsaking our friends. They stand against us, because we stand in their way.

We are not deceived by their pretenses to piety. We have seen their kind before. They are the heirs of all the murderous ideologies of the 20th century. By sacrificing human life to serve their radical visions—by abandoning every value except the will to power—they follow in the path of fascism, Nazism, and totalitarianism. And they will follow that path all the way, to where it ends: in history's unmarked grave of discarded lies.

Americans are asking: How will we fight and win this war? We will direct every resource at our command—every means of diplomacy, every tool of intelligence, every instrument of law enforcement, every financial influence, and every necessary weapon of war—to the disruption and to the defeat of the global terror network.

Now this war will not be like the war against Iraq a decade ago, with a decisive liberation of territory and a swift conclusion. It will not look like the air war above Kosovo two years ago, where no ground troops were used and not a single American was lost in combat.

Our response involves far more than instant retaliation and isolated strikes. Americans should not expect one battle, but a lengthy campaign, unlike any other we have ever seen. It may include dramatic strikes, visible on TV, and covert operations, secret even in success. We will starve terrorists of funding, turn them one against another, drive them from place to place, until there is no refuge or no rest. And we will pursue nations that provide aid or safe haven to terrorism. Every nation, in every region, now has a decision to make. Either you are with us, or you are with the terrorists. From this day forward, any nation that continues to harbor or support terrorism will be regarded by the United States as a hostile regime.

Our nation has been put on notice: We are not immune from attack. We will take defensive measures against terrorism to protect Americans. Today, dozens of federal departments and agencies, as well as state and local governments, have responsibilities affecting homeland security. These efforts must be coordinated at the highest level. So tonight I announce the creation of a Cabinet-level position reporting directly to me—the Office of Homeland Security.

And tonight I also announce a distinguished American to lead this effort, to strengthen American security: a military veteran, an effective governor, a true patriot, a trusted friend—Pennsylvania's Tom Ridge. He will lead, oversee, and coordinate a comprehensive national strategy to safeguard our country against terrorism, and respond to any attacks that may come.

These measures are essential. But the only way to defeat terrorism as a threat to our way of life is to stop it, eliminate it, and destroy it where it grows. Many will be involved in this effort, from FBI agents to intelligence operatives to the reservists we have called to active duty. All deserve our thanks, and all have our prayers. And tonight, a few miles from the damaged Pentagon, I have a message for our military: Be ready. I've called the Armed Forces to alert, and there is a reason. The hour is coming when America will act, and you will make us proud.

This is not, however, just America's fight. And what is at stake is not just America's freedom. This is the world's fight. This is civilization's fight. This is the fight of all who believe in progress and pluralism, tolerance, and freedom.

We ask every nation to join us. We will ask, and we will need, the help of police forces, intelligence services, and banking systems around the world. The United States is grateful that many nations and many international organizations have already responded—with sympathy and with support. Nations from Latin America, to Asia, to Africa, to Europe, to the Islamic world. Perhaps the NATO Charter reflects best the attitude of the world: An attack on one is an attack on all.

The civilized world is rallying to America's side. They understand that if this terror goes unpunished, their own cities, their own citizens may be next. Terror, unanswered, cannot only bring down buildings, it can threaten the stability of legitimate governments. And you know what—we're not going to allow it.

Americans are asking: What is expected of us? I ask you to live your lives, and hug your children. I know many citizens have fears tonight, and I ask you to be calm and resolute, even in the face of a continuing threat.

I ask you to uphold the values of America, and remember why so many have come here. We are in a fight for our principles, and our first responsibility is to live by them. No one should be singled out for unfair treatment or unkind words because of their ethnic background or religious faith.

I ask you to continue to support the victims of this tragedy with your contributions. Those who want to give can go to a central source of information, libertyunites.org, to find the names of groups providing direct help in New York, Pennsylvania, and Virginia.

The thousands of FBI agents who are now at work in this investigation may need your cooperation, and I ask you to give it.

I ask for your patience, with the delays and inconveniences that may accompany tighter security; and for your patience in what will be a long struggle.

I ask your continued participation and confidence in the American economy. Terrorists attacked a symbol of American prosperity. They did not touch its source. America is successful because of the hard work, and creativity, and enterprise of our people. These were the true strengths of our economy before September 11th, and they are our strengths today.

And, finally, please continue praying for the victims of terror and their families, for those in uniform, and for our great country. Prayer has comforted us in sorrow, and will help strengthen us for the journey ahead.

Tonight I thank my fellow Americans for what you have already done and for what you will do. And ladies and gentlemen of the Congress, I thank you, their representatives, for what you have already done and for what we will do together.

Tonight, we face new and sudden national challenges. We will come together to improve air safety, to dramatically expand the number of air marshals on domestic flights, and take new measures to prevent hijacking. We will come together to promote stability and keep our airlines flying, with direct assistance during this emergency.

We will come together to give law enforcement the additional tools it needs to track down terror here at home. We will come together to strengthen our intelligence capabilities to know the plans of terrorists before they act, and to find them before they strike.

We will come together to take active steps that strengthen America's economy, and put our people back to work.

Tonight we welcome two leaders who embody the extraordinary spirit of all New Yorkers: Governor George Pataki, and Mayor Rudolph Giuliani. As a symbol of America's resolve, my administration will work with Congress, and these two leaders, to show the world that we will rebuild New York City.

After all that has just passed—all the lives taken, and all the possibilities and hopes that died with them—it is natural to wonder if America's future is one of fear. Some speak of an age of terror. I know there are struggles ahead, and dangers to face. But this country will define our times, not be defined by them. As long as the United States of America is determined and strong, this will not be an age of terror; this will be an age of liberty, here and across the world.

Great harm has been done to us. We have suffered great loss. And in our grief and anger we have found our mission and our moment. Freedom and fear are at war. The advance of human freedom—the great achievement of our time, and the great hope of every time—now depends on us. Our nation—this generation—will lift a dark threat of violence from our people and our future. We will rally the world to this cause by our efforts, by our courage. We will not tire, we will not falter, and we will not fail.

It is my hope that in the months and years ahead, life will return almost to normal. We'll go back to our lives and routines, and that is good. Even grief recedes with time and grace. But our resolve must not pass. Each of us will remember what happened that day, and to whom it happened. We'll remember the moment the news came—where we were and what we were doing. Some will remember an image of a fire, or a story of rescue. Some will carry memories of a face and a voice gone forever.

And I will carry this: It is the police shield of a man named George Howard, who died at the World Trade Center trying to save others. It was given to me by his mom, Arlene, as a proud memorial to her son. This is my reminder of lives that ended, and a task that does not end.

I will not forget this wound to our country or those who inflicted it. I will not yield; I will not rest; I will not relent in waging this struggle for freedom and security for the American people.

The course of this conflict is not known, yet its outcome is certain. Freedom and fear, justice and cruelty, have always been at war, and we know that God is not neutral between them.

Fellow citizens, we'll meet violence with patient justice—assured of the rightness of our cause, and confident of the victories to come. In all that lies before us, may God grant us wisdom, and may He watch over the United States of America.

Thank you.

Notes

1. David Zarefsky, "George W. Bush Discovers Rhetoric: September 20, 2001, and the U.S. Response to Terrorism," in *The Ethos of Rhetoric,* ed. Michael J. Hyde, 136–55 (Columbia: University of South Carolina Press, 2004), 152.

2. Dan Balz and Bob Woodward, "A Presidency Defined in One Speech," *Washington Post,* February 2, 2002, A01.

3. Ibid.

Charles Krauthammer

"A Unipolar World"

FEBRUARY 20, 2004

The American Enterprise Institute's

Irving Kristol Award Lecture

CHARLES KRAUTHAMMER was born in New York City and raised in Montreal. He attended McGill University, where he majored in political science and economics before studying at Oxford University where he was the Commonwealth Scholar in Politics. In 1975, he was awarded his MD from Harvard University and practiced medicine for three years before serving as the chief resident in psychiatry at Massachusetts General Hospital. This position would serve as a stepping-stone to his next post as director of psychiatric research for the Carter administration.

During this period Krauthammer began writing articles for the *New Republic*. Soon thereafter his powerful polemics caught the attention of members of Vice President Walter Mondale's staff. Thus in 1980 he became a speechwriter for Walter Mondale's bid for the presidency; hardly the background one might expect from a member of the American conservative movement. But Krauthammer, who is often labeled a "neoconservative," is quite typical for those so called.

Neoconservatism remains one of the most misappropriated terms in politics today. James Q. Wilson offers clarity on the subject:

Neoconservatism is an awkward and not very accurate name for an attitude that holds social reality to be complex and change difficult. If there is any article of faith common to almost every adherent, it is the Law of Unintended Consequences. Things never work out quite as you hope; in particular, government programs often do not achieve their objectives or do achieve them but with high or unexpected costs. A true conservative may oppose change because it upsets the accumulated wisdom of tradition or the legacy of history; a neoconservative questions change because, though present circumstances are bad and something ought to be done, it is necessary to do that something cautiously, experimentally, and with a minimum of bureaucratic authority. Neoconservatives, accordingly, place a lot of stock in applied social science research.[1]

Indeed, many neoconservatives are disaffected former liberals, often from academe or intellectual circles.

Today, Krauthammer writes for *Time* magazine, the *Weekly Standard*, and is a frequent guest on the Fox News Channel. He is the recipient of some of the most prestigious awards in political writing, including the Pulitzer Prize for Distinguished Commentary.

In 2004, the American Enterprise Institute awarded Krauthammer the Irving Kristol Award, an award named after the man most consider the "father of neonconservatism." The following speech was Krauthammer's keynote speech delivered after receiving the award. In it he asserts that the fall of the former Soviet Union made America a "unipolar power." The speech entertains a central question: In a post-9/11 world, "what is a unipolar power to do?" In offering his answer Krauthammer dismisses the classic dichotomy between idealism and realism. Instead, he argues that the United States must pursue a third path—that of "democratic globalism" which he believes is not Wilsonian (idealism) in nature and represents "an improvement over realism."

According to Krauthammer, spreading democracy and liberty is an indispensable means for securing American interests because "Democracies are inherently more friendly to the United States, less belligerent to their neighbors, and generally more inclined to peace."

"A Unipolar World" is, in many ways, an exposition of President George W. Bush's post-9/11 foreign policy stance. Indeed, Bush's second inaugural echoes many of the themes Krauthammer explicates, and thus represents a significant development in the history of the American conservative movement.

Delivered February 20, 2004, in Washington, DC

Americans have a healthy aversion to foreign policy. It stems from a sense of thrift: Who needs it? We're protected by two great oceans, we have this continent practically to ourselves and we share it with just two neighbors, both friendly, one so friendly that its people seem intent upon moving in with us. It took three giants of the twentieth century to drag us into its great battles: Wilson into World War I, Roosevelt into World War II, Truman into the Cold War. And then it ended with one of the great anti-climaxes in history. Without a shot fired, without a revolution, without so much as a press release, the Soviet Union simply gave up and disappeared. It was the end of everything—the end of communism, of socialism, of the Cold War, of the European wars. But the end of everything was also a beginning. On December 26, 1991, the Soviet Union died and something new was born, something utterly new—a unipolar world dominated by a single superpower unchecked by any rival and with decisive reach in every corner of the globe. This is a staggering new development in history, not seen since the fall of Rome. It is so new, so strange, that we have no idea how to deal with it. Our first reaction—the 1990s—was utter confusion. The next reaction was awe. When Paul Kennedy, who had once popularized the idea of American decline, saw what America did in the Afghan war—a display of fully mobilized, furiously concentrated unipolar power at a distance of 8,000 miles—he not only recanted, he stood in wonder: "Nothing has ever existed like this disparity of power;" he wrote, "nothing. . . . No other nation comes close. . . . Charlemagne's empire was merely western European in its reach. The Roman empire stretched farther afield, but there was another great empire in Persia, and a larger one in China. There is, therefore, no comparison." Even Rome is no model for what America is today. First, because we do not have the imperial culture of Rome. We are an Athenian republic, even more republican and infinitely more democratic than Athens. And this American Republic has acquired the largest seeming empire in the history of the world—acquired it in a fit of absent-mindedness greater even than Britain's. And it was not just absent-mindedness; it was sheer inadvertence. We got here because of Europe's suicide in the world wars of the twentieth century, and then the death of its Eurasian successor, Soviet Russia, for having adopted a political and economic system so inhuman that, like a genetically defective organism, it simply expired in its sleep. Leaving us with global dominion.

Second, we are unlike Rome, unlike Britain and France and Spain and the other classical empires of modern times, in that we do not hunger for territory. The use of the word "empire" in the American context is ridiculous. It is absurd to apply the word to a people whose first instinct upon arriving on anyone's soil is to demand an exit strategy. I can assure you that when the Romans went into Gaul and the British into India, they were not looking for exit strategies. They were looking for entry strategies. In David Lean's *Lawrence of Arabia*, King Faisal says to Lawrence: "I think you are another of these desert-loving English. . . . The English have a great hunger for desolate places." Indeed, for five centuries, the Europeans did hunger for deserts and jungles and oceans and new continents. Americans do not. We like it here. We like our McDonalds. We like our football. We like our rock-and-roll. We've got the Grand Canyon and Graceland. We've got Silicon Valley and South Beach. We've got everything. And if that's not enough, we've got Vegas, which is a facsimile of everything. What could we possibly need anywhere else? We don't like exotic climates.

We don't like exotic languages—lots of declensions and moods. We don't even know what a mood is. We like Iowa corn and New York hot dogs, and if we want Chinese or Indian or Italian, we go to the food court. We don't send the Marines for takeout. That's because we are not an imperial power. We are a commercial republic. We don't take food; we trade for it. Which makes us something unique in history, an anomaly, a hybrid: a commercial republic with overwhelming global power. A commercial republic that, by pure accident of history, has been designated custodian of the international system. The eyes of every supplicant from East Timor to Afghanistan, from Iraq to Liberia; Arab and Israeli, Irish and British, North and South Korean are upon us. That is who we are. That is where we are. Now the question is: What do we do? What is a unipolar power to do? The oldest and most venerable answer is to hoard that power and retreat. This is known as isolationism. Of all the foreign policy schools in America, it has the oldest pedigree, not surprising in the only great power in history to be isolated by two vast oceans.

Isolationism originally sprang from a view of America as spiritually superior to the Old World. We were too good to be corrupted by its low intrigues, entangled by its cynical alliances.

Today, however, isolationism is an ideology of fear. Fear of trade. Fear of immigrants. Fear of the Other. Isolationists want to cut off trade and immigration, and withdraw from our military and strategic commitments around the world. Even isolationists, of course, did not oppose the war in Afghanistan, because it was so obviously an act of self-defense—only a fool or a knave or a Susan Sontag could oppose that. But anything beyond that, isolationists oppose. They are for a radical retrenchment of American power—for pulling up the drawbridge to Fortress America. Isolationism is an important school of thought historically, but not today. Not just because of its brutal intellectual reductionism, but because it is so obviously inappropriate to the world of today—a world of export-driven economies, of massive population flows, and of 9/11, the definitive demonstration that the combination of modern technology and transnational primitivism has erased the barrier between "over there" and over here.

Classical isolationism is not just intellectually obsolete; it is politically bankrupt as well. Four years ago, its most public advocate, Pat Buchanan, ran for president of the United States, and carried Palm Beach. By accident.

Classic isolationism is moribund and marginalized. Who then rules America? In the 1990s, it was liberal internationalism. Liberal internationalism is the foreign policy of the Democratic Party and the religion of the foreign policy elite. It has a peculiar history. It traces its pedigree to Woodrow Wilson's utopianism, Harry Truman's anticommunism, and John Kennedy's militant universalism. But after the Vietnam War, it was transmuted into an ideology of passivity, acquiescence and almost reflexive anti-interventionism.

Liberals today proudly take credit for Truman's and Kennedy's roles in containing communism, but they prefer to forget that, for the last half of the Cold War, liberals used "cold warrior" as an epithet. In the early 1980s, they gave us the nuclear freeze movement, a form of unilateral disarmament in the face of Soviet nuclear advances. Today, John Kerry boasts of opposing, during the 1980s, what he calls Ronald Reagan's "illegal war in Central America"—and oppose he did what was, in fact, an indigenous anticommunist rebellion that ultimately succeeded in bringing down Sandinista rule and ushering in democracy in all of Central America. That boast reminds us how militant was liberal passivity in the last half of the Cold War. But that passivity outlived the Cold War. When Kuwait was invaded, the question was: Should the United States go to war to prevent the Persian Gulf from falling into hostile hands? The Democratic Party joined the Buchananite isolationists in saying No. The Democrats voted No overwhelmingly—two to one in the House, more than four to one in the Senate. And yet, quite astonishingly, when liberal internationalism came to power just two years later in the form of the Clinton administration, it turned almost hyperinterventionist. It involved us four times in military action: deepening intervention in Somalia, invading Haiti, bombing Bosnia, and finally going to war over Kosovo. How to explain the amazing transmutation of Cold War and Gulf War doves into Haiti and Balkan hawks? The crucial and obvious difference is this: Haiti, Bosnia, and Kosovo were humanitarian ventures—fights for right and good, devoid of raw national interest. And only humanitarian interventionism—disinterested interventionism devoid of national interest—is morally pristine enough to justify the use of force. The history of the 1990s refutes the lazy notion that liberals have an aversion to the use of force. They do not. They have an aversion to using force for reasons of pure national interest. And by national interest I do not mean simple self-defense. Everyone believes in self-defense, as in Afghanistan. I am talking about national interest as defined by a Great Power: shaping the international environment by projecting power abroad to secure economic, political, and strategic goods. Intervening militarily for that kind of national interest, liberal internationalism finds unholy and unsupportable. It sees that kind of national interest as merely self-interest writ large, in effect, a form of grand national selfishness. Hence Kuwait, no; Kosovo, yes. The other defining feature of the Clinton foreign policy was multilateralism, which expressed itself in a mania for treaties. The Clinton administration negotiated a dizzying succession of parchment promises on bio weapons, chemical weapons, nuclear testing, carbon emissions, anti-ballistic missiles, etc. Why? No sentient being could believe that, say, the chemical or biological weapons treaties were anything more than transparently useless. Senator Joseph Biden once defended the Chemical Weapons Convention, which even its proponents admitted was unenforceable, on the grounds that it would "provide us with a valuable tool"—the "moral suasion of the entire international community."

Moral suasion? Was it moral suasion that made Qaddafi see the wisdom of giving up his weapons of mass destruction? Or Iran agree for the first time to spot nuclear inspections? It was the suasion of the bayonet. It was the ignominious fall of Saddam—and the desire of interested spectators not to be next on the list. The whole point of this treaty was to keep rogue states from developing chemical weapons. Rogue states are, by definition, impervious to moral suasion.

Moral suasion is a farce. Why then this obsession with conventions, protocols, legalisms? Their obvious net effect is to temper American power. Who, after all, was really going to be most constrained by these treaties? The ABM amendments were aimed squarely at American advances and strategic defenses, not at Russia, which lags hopelessly behind. The Kyoto Protocol exempted India and China. The nuclear test ban would have seriously degraded the American nuclear arsenal. And the landmine treaty (which the Clinton administration spent months negotiating but, in the end, met so much Pentagon resistance that even Clinton could not initial it) would have had a devastating impact on U.S. conventional forces, particularly at the DMZ in Korea.

But that, you see, is the whole point of the multilateral enterprise: To reduce American freedom of action by making it subservient to, dependent on, constricted by the will—and interests—of other nations. To tie down Gulliver with a thousand strings. To domesticate the most undomesticated, most outsized, national interest on the planet: ours.

Today, multilateralism remains the overriding theme of liberal internationalism. When in power in the 1990s, multilateralism expressed itself as a mania for treaties. When out of power in this decade, multilateralism manifests itself in the slavish pursuit of "international legitimacy"—and opposition to any American action undertaken without universal foreign blessing. Which is why the Democratic critique of the war in Iraq is so peculiarly one of process and not of policy. The problem was that we did not have the permission of the UN; we did not have a large enough coalition; we did not have a second Security Council resolution. Kofi Annan was unhappy and the French were cross. The Democratic presidential candidates all say that we should have internationalized the conflict, brought in the UN, enlisted the allies. Why? Two reasons: assistance and legitimacy. First, they say, we could have used these other countries to help us in the reconstruction. This is rich. Everyone would like to have more help in reconstruction. It would be lovely to have the Germans and the French helping reconstruct Baghdad. But the question is moot, and the argument is cynical: France and Germany made absolutely clear that they would never support the overthrow of Saddam. So, accommodating them was not a way to get them into the reconstruction, it was a way to ensure that there would never be any reconstruction, because Saddam would still be in power. Of course it would be nice if we had more allies rather than fewer. It would also be nice to be able to fly. But when some nations are not with you on your enterprise, including them in your coalition is not a way to broaden it; it's a way to abolish it. At which point, liberal internationalists switch gears and appeal to legitimacy—on the grounds that multilateral action has a higher moral standing. I have always found this line of argument incomprehensible. By what possible moral calculus does an American intervention to liberate 25 million people forfeit moral legitimacy because it lacks the blessing of the butchers of Tiananmen Square or the cynics of the Quai d'Orsay? Which is why it is hard to take these arguments at face value. Look: We know why liberal internationalists demanded UN sanction for the war in Iraq. It was a way to stop the war. It was the Gulliver effect. Call a committee meeting of countries with hostile or contrary interests (i.e., the Security Council) and you have guaranteed yourself another twelve years of inaction. Historically, multilateralism is a way for weak countries to multiply their power by attaching themselves to stronger ones. But multilateralism imposed on Great Powers, and particularly on a unipolar power, is intended to restrain that power. Which is precisely why France is an ardent multilateralist. But why should America be? Why, in the end, does liberal internationalism want to tie down Gulliver, to blunt the pursuit of American national interests by making them subordinate to a myriad of other interests?

In the immediate post-Vietnam era, this aversion to national interest might have been attributed to self-doubt and self-loathing. I don't know. What I do know is that today it is a mistake to see liberal foreign policy as deriving from anti-Americanism or lack of patriotism or a late efflorescence of 1960s radicalism. On the contrary. The liberal aversion to national interest stems from an idealism, a larger vision of country, a vision of some ambition and nobility—the ideal of a true international community. And that is: To transform the international system from the Hobbesian universe into a Lockean universe. To turn the state of nature into a norm-driven community. To turn the law of the jungle into the rule of law—of treaties and contracts and UN resolutions. In short, to remake the international system in the image of domestic civil society.

They dream of a new world, a world described in 1943 by Cordell Hull, FDR's secretary of state—a world in which "there will no longer be need for spheres of influence, for alliances, for balance of power, or any other of the special arrangements by which, in the unhappy past, the nations strove to safeguard their security or promote their interests." And to create such a true international community, you have to temper, transcend, and, in the end, abolish the very idea of state power and national interest. Hence the antipathy to American hegemony and American power. If you are going to break the international arena to the mold of domestic society, you have to domesticate its single most powerful actor. You have to abolish American dominance, not only as an affront to fairness, but also as the greatest obstacle on the whole planet to a democratized international system where all live under self-governing international institutions and self-enforcing international norms.

This vision is all very nice. All very noble. And all very crazy. Which brings us to the third great foreign policy school: realism. The realist looks at this great liberal project and sees a hopeless illusion. Because turning the Hobbesian world that has existed since long before the Peloponnesian Wars into a Lockean world, turning a jungle into a suburban subdivision, requires a revolution in human nature. Not just an erector set of new institutions, but a revolution in human nature. And realists do not believe in revolutions in human nature, much less stake their future, and the future of their nation, on them.

Realism recognizes the fundamental fallacy in the whole idea of the international system being modeled on domestic society. First, what holds domestic society together is a supreme central authority wielding a monopoly of power and enforcing norms. In the international arena there is no such thing. Domestic society may look like a place of self-regulating norms, but if somebody breaks into your house, you call 911, and the police arrive with guns drawn. That's not exactly self-enforcement. That's law enforcement.

Second, domestic society rests on the shared goodwill, civility, and common values of its individual members. What values are shared by, say, Britain, Cuba, Yemen, and Zimbabwe—all nominal members of this fiction we call the "international community"? Of course, you can have smaller communities of shared interests—NAFTA, ANZUS, or the European Union. But the European conceit that relations with all nations—regardless of ideology, regardless of culture, regardless even of open hostility—should be transacted on the EU model of suasion and norms and negotiations and solemn contractual agreements is an illusion. A fisheries treaty with Canada is something real. An Agreed Framework on plutonium processing with the likes of North Korea is not worth the paper it is written on. The realist believes the definition of peace Ambrose Bierce offered in The Devil's Dictionary: "Peace: noun, in international affairs, a period of cheating between two periods of fighting."

Hence the Realist axiom: The "international community" is a fiction. It is not a community, it is a cacophony—of straining ambitions, disparate values and contending power.

What does hold the international system together? What keeps it from degenerating into total anarchy? Not the phony security of treaties, not the best of goodwill among the nicer nations. In the unipolar world we inhabit, what stability we do enjoy today is owed to the overwhelming power and deterrent threat of the United States.

If someone invades your house, you call the cops. Who do you call if someone invades your country? You dial Washington. In the unipolar world, the closest thing to a centralized authority, to an enforcer of norms, is America—American power. And ironically, American power is precisely what liberal internationalism wants to constrain and tie down and subsume in pursuit of some brave new Lockean world. Realists do not live just in America. I found one in Finland. During the 1997 negotiations in Oslo over the land mine treaty, one of the rare holdouts, interestingly enough, was Finland. The Finnish prime minister stoutly opposed the land mine ban. And for that he was scolded by his Scandinavian neighbors. To which he responded tartly that this was a "very convenient" pose for the "other Nordic countries"—after all, Finland is their land mine.

Finland is the land mine between Russia and Scandinavia. America is the land mine between barbarism and civilization. Where would South Korea be without America and its landmines along the DMZ? Where would Europe—with its cozy arrogant community—be without America having saved it from the Soviet colossus? Where would the Middle East be had American power not stopped Saddam in 1991?

The land mine that protects civilization from barbarism is not parchment but power, and in a unipolar world, American power—wielded, if necessary, unilaterally. If necessary, preemptively.

Now, those uneasy with American power have made these two means of wielding it—preemption and unilateralism—the focus of unrelenting criticism. The doctrine of preemption, in particular, has been widely attacked for violating international norms.

CHARLES KRAUTHAMMER

What international norm? The one under which Israel was universally condemned—even the Reagan Administration joined the condemnation at the Security Council—for preemptively destroying Iraq's Osirak nuclear reactor in 1981? Does anyone today doubt that it was the right thing to do, both strategically and morally?

In a world of terrorists, terrorist states and weapons of mass destruction, the option of preemption is especially necessary. In the bipolar world of the Cold War, with a stable non-suicidal adversary, deterrence could work. Deterrence does not work against people who ache for heaven. It does not work against undeterrables. And it does not work against undetectables: nonsuicidal enemy regimes that might attack through clandestine means—a suitcase nuke or anonymously delivered anthrax. Against both undeterrables and undetectables, preemption is the only possible strategy.

Moreover, the doctrine of preemption against openly hostile states pursuing weapons of mass destruction is an improvement on classical deterrence. Traditionally, we deterred the use of WMDs by the threat of retaliation after we'd been attacked—and that's too late; the point of preemption is to deter the very acquisition of WMDs in the first place.

Whether or not Iraq had large stockpiles of WMDs, the very fact that the United States overthrew a hostile regime that repeatedly refused to come clean on its weapons has had precisely this deterrent effect. We are safer today not just because Saddam is gone, but because Libya and any others contemplating trafficking with WMDs, have—for the first time—seen that it carries a cost, a very high cost.

Yes, of course, imperfect intelligence makes preemption problematic. But that is not an objection on principle, it is an objection in practice. Indeed, the objection concedes the principle. We need good intelligence. But we remain defenseless if we abjure the option of preemption.

The other great objection to the way American unipolar power has been wielded is its unilateralism. I would dispute how unilateralist we have in fact been. Constructing ad hoc "coalitions of the willing" hardly qualifies as unilateralism just because they do not have a secretariat in Brussels or on the East River.

Moreover, unilateralism is often the very road to multilateralism. As we learned from the Gulf War, it is the leadership of the United States—indeed, its willingness to act unilaterally if necessary—that galvanized the Gulf War coalition into existence. Without the president of the United States declaring "This will not stand" about the invasion of Kuwait—and making it clear that America would go it alone if it had to—there never would have been the great wall-to-wall coalition that is now so retroactively applauded and held up as a model of multilateralism.

Of course one acts in concert with others if possible. It is nice when others join us in the breach. No one seeks to be unilateral. Unilateralism simply means that one does not allow oneself to be held hostage to the will of others.

Of course you build coalitions when possible. In 2003, we garnered a coalition of the willing for Iraq that included substantial allies like Britain, Australia, Spain, Italy, and much of Eastern Europe. France and Germany made clear from the beginning that they would never join in the overthrow of Saddam. Therefore the choice was not a wide coalition versus a narrow one, but a narrow coalition versus none. There were serious arguments against war in Iraq—but the fact France did not approve was not one of them.

Irving Kristol once explained that he preferred the Organization of American States to the United Nations because in the OAS we can be voted down in only three languages, thereby saving translators' fees. Realists choose not to be Gulliver. In an international system with no sovereign, no police, no protection—where power is the ultimate arbiter and history has bequeathed us unprecedented power—we should be vigilant in preserving that power. And our freedom of action to use it.

But here we come up against the limits of realism: you cannot live by power alone. Realism is a valuable antidote to the woolly internationalism of the 1990s. But realism can only take you so far.

Its basic problem lies in its definition of national interest as classically offered by its great theorist, Hans Morgenthau: Interest defined as power. Morgenthau postulated that what drives nations, what motivates their foreign policy, is the will to power—to keep it and expand it.

For most Americans, will to power might be a correct description of the world—of what motivates other countries—but it cannot be a prescription for America. It cannot be our purpose. America cannot and will not live by realpolitik alone. Our foreign policy must be driven by something beyond power. Unless conservatives present ideals to challenge the liberal ideal of a domesticated international community, they will lose the debate.

Which is why among American conservatives, another, more idealistic, school has arisen that sees America's national interest as an expression of values.

It is this fourth school that has guided U.S. foreign policy in this decade. This conservative alternative to realism is often lazily and invidiously called neoconservatism, but that is a very odd name for a school whose major proponents in the world today are George W. Bush and Tony Blair—if they are neoconservatives, then Margaret Thatcher was a liberal. There's nothing neo about Bush, and there's nothing con about Blair.

Yet they are the principal proponents today of what might be called democratic globalism, a foreign policy that defines the national interest not as power but as values, and that identifies one supreme value, what John Kennedy called "the success of liberty." As President Bush put it in his speech at Whitehall last November: "The United States and Great Britain share a mission in the world beyond the balance of power or the simple pursuit of interest. We seek the advance of freedom and the peace that freedom brings."

Beyond power. Beyond interest. Beyond interest defined as power. That is the credo of democratic globalism. Which explains its political appeal: America is a nation uniquely built not on blood, race or consanguinity, but on a proposition—to which its sacred honor has been pledged for two centuries. This American exceptionalism explains why non-Americans find this foreign policy so difficult to credit; why Blair has had more difficulty garnering support for it in his country; and why Europe, in particular, finds this kind of value-driven foreign policy hopelessly and irritatingly moralistic.

Democratic globalism sees as the engine of history not the will to power but the will to freedom. And while it has been attacked as a dreamy, idealistic innovation, its inspiration comes from the Truman Doctrine of 1947, the Kennedy inaugural of 1961, and Reagan's "Evil Empire" speech of 1983. They all sought to recast a struggle for power between two geopolitical titans into a struggle between freedom and unfreedom, and yes, good and evil.

Which is why the Truman Doctrine was heavily criticized by realists like Hans Morgenthau and George Kennan—and Reagan was vilified by the entire foreign policy establishment: for the sin of ideologizing the Cold War by injecting a moral overlay.

That was then. Today, post-9/11, we find ourselves in a similar existential struggle but with a different enemy: not Soviet communism, but Arab-Islamic totalitarianism, both secular and religious. Bush and Blair are similarly attacked for naïvely and crudely casting this struggle as one of freedom versus unfreedom, good versus evil.

Now, given the way not just freedom but human decency were suppressed in both Afghanistan and Iraq, the two major battles of this new war, you would have to give Bush and Blair's moral claims the decided advantage of being obviously true. Nonetheless, something can be true and still be dangerous. Many people are deeply uneasy with the Bush-Blair doctrine—many conservatives in particular. When Blair declares in his address to Congress: "The spread of freedom is . . . our last line of defense and our first line of attack," they see a dangerously expansive, aggressively utopian foreign policy. In short, they see Woodrow Wilson.

Now, to a conservative, Woodrow Wilson is fightin' words. Yes, this vision is expansive and perhaps utopian. But it ain't Wilsonian. Wilson envisioned the spread of democratic values through as-yet-to-be invented international

CHARLES KRAUTHAMMER

institutions. He could be forgiven for that. In 1918, there was no way to know how utterly corrupt and useless those international institutions would turn out to be. Eight decades of bitter experience later—with Libya chairing the UN Commission on Human Rights—there is no way not to know.

Democratic globalism is not Wilsonian. Its attractiveness is precisely that it shares realism's insights about the centrality of power. Its attractiveness is precisely that it has appropriate contempt for the fictional legalisms of liberal internationalism. Moreover, democratic globalism is an improvement over realism. What it can teach realism is that the spread of democracy is not just an end but a means, an indispensable means for securing American interests. The reason is simple. Democracies are inherently more friendly to the United States, less belligerent to their neighbors, and generally more inclined to peace. Realists are right that to protect your interests, you often have to go around the world bashing bad guys over the head. But that technique, no matter how satisfying, has its limits. At some point, you have to implant something, something organic and self-developing. And that something is democracy. But where? The danger of democratic globalism is its universalism, its open-ended commitment to human freedom, its temptation to plant the flag of democracy everywhere. It must learn to say no. And indeed, it does say no. But when it says no to Liberia, or Congo, or Burma, or countenances alliances with authoritarian rulers in places like Pakistan or, for that matter, Russia, it stands accused of hypocrisy. Which is why we must articulate criteria for saying yes.

Where to intervene? Where to bring democracy? Where to nation-build? I propose a single criterion: Where it counts.

Call it democratic realism. And this is its axiom: We will support democracy everywhere, but we will commit blood and treasure only in places where there is a strategic necessity—meaning, places central to the larger war against the existential enemy, the enemy that poses a global mortal threat to freedom. Where does it count? Fifty years ago, Germany and Japan counted. Why? Because they were the seeds of the greatest global threat to freedom in mid-century—fascism—and then were turned, by nation building, into bulwarks against the next great threat to freedom, Soviet communism.

Where does it count today? Where the overthrow of radicalism and the beginnings of democracy can have a decisive effect in the war against the new global threat to freedom, the new existential enemy, the Arab-Islamic totalitarianism that has threatened us in both its secular and religious forms for the quarter-century since the Khomeini revolution of 1979.

Establishing civilized, decent, nonbelligerent, pro-Western polities in Afghanistan and Iraq and ultimately their key neighbors would, like the flipping of Germany and Japan in the 1940s, change the strategic balance in the fight against Arab-Islamic radicalism.

Yes, it may be a bridge too far. Realists have been warning against the hubris of thinking we can transform an alien culture because of some postulated natural and universal human will to freedom. And they may yet be right. But how do they know in advance? Half a century ago, we heard the same confident warnings about the imperviousness to democracy of Confucian culture. That proved stunningly wrong. Where is it written that Arabs are incapable of democracy?

Yes, as in Germany and Japan, the undertaking is enormous, ambitious and arrogant. It may yet fail. But we cannot afford not to try. There is not a single, remotely plausible, alternative strategy for attacking the monster behind 9/11. It's not Osama bin Laden; it is the cauldron of political oppression, religious intolerance, and social ruin in the Arab-Islamic world—oppression transmuted and deflected by regimes with no legitimacy into virulent, murderous anti-Americanism. It's not one man; it is a condition. It will be nice to find that man and hang him, but that's the cops-and-robbers law-enforcement model of fighting terrorism that we tried for twenty years and that gave us 9/11. This is war, and in war arresting murderers is nice. But you win by taking

CHARLES KRAUTHAMMER

territory—and leaving something behind. We are the unipolar power and what do we do?

In August 1900, David Hilbert gave a speech to the International Congress of Mathematicians naming twenty-three still-unsolved mathematical problems bequeathed by the nineteenth century to the twentieth. Had he presented the great unsolved geopolitical problems bequeathed to the twentieth century, one would have stood out above all: the rise of Germany and its accommodation within the European state system.

Similarly today, at the dawn of the twenty-first century, we can see clearly the two great geopolitical challenges on the horizon: the inexorable rise of China and the coming demographic collapse of Europe, both of which will irrevocably disequilibrate the international system.

But those problems come later. They are for mid-century. They are for the next generation. And that generation will not even get to these problems unless we first deal with our problem.

And our problem is 9/11 and the roots of Arab-Islamic nihilism. September 11 felt like a new problem, but for all its shock and surprise, it is an old problem with a new face. September 11 felt like the initiation of a new history, but it was a return to history, the twentieth century history of radical ideologies and existential enemies.

The anomaly is not the world of today. The anomaly was the 1990s, our holiday from history. It felt like peace, but it was an interval of dreaming between two periods of reality.

From which 9/11 awoke us. It startled us into thinking everything was new. It's not. What is new is what happened not on 9/11, but ten years earlier on December 26, 1991, the emergence of the United States as the world's unipolar power. What is unique is our advantage in this struggle, an advantage we did not have during the struggles of the twentieth century. The question for our time is how to press this advantage, how to exploit our unipolar power, how to deploy it to win the old/new war that exploded upon us on 9/11.

What is the unipolar power to do? Four schools, four answers.

The isolationists want simply to ignore unipolarity, pull up the drawbridge, and defend Fortress America. Alas, the Fortress has no moat—not after the airplane, the submarine, the ballistic missile—and as for the drawbridge, it was blown up on 9/11. Then there are the liberal internationalists. They like to dream, and to the extent they are aware of our unipolar power, they don't like it. They see its use for anything other than humanitarianism or reflexive self-defense as an expression of national selfishness. And they don't just want us to ignore our unique power, they want us to yield it piece by piece, by subsuming ourselves in a new global architecture in which America becomes not the arbiter of international events, but a good and tame international citizen.

Then there is realism, which has the clearest understanding of the new unipolarity and its uses—unilateral and preemptive if necessary. But in the end, it fails because it offers no vision. It is all means and no ends. It cannot adequately define our mission.

Hence, the fourth school: democratic globalism. It has, in this decade, rallied the American people to a struggle over values. It seeks to vindicate the American idea by making the spread of democracy, the success of liberty, the ends and means of American foreign policy.

I support that. I applaud that. But I believe it must be tempered in its universalistic aspirations and rhetoric from a democratic globalism to a democratic realism. It must be targeted, focused and limited. We are friends to all, but we come ashore only where it really counts. And where it counts today is that Islamic crescent stretching from North Africa to Afghanistan. In October 1962, during the Cuban Missile crisis, we came to the edge of the abyss. Then, accompanied by our equally shaken adversary, we both deliberately drew back. On September 11, 2001, we saw the face of Armageddon again, but this time with an enemy that does not draw back. This time the enemy knows no reason.

　　　　　　　　　　　CHARLES KRAUTHAMMER

Were that the only difference between now and then, our situation would be hopeless. But there is a second difference between now and then: the uniqueness of our power, unrivaled, not just today but ever. That evens the odds. The rationality of the enemy is something beyond our control. But the use of our power is within our control. And if that power is used wisely, constrained not by illusions and fictions but only by the limits of our mission—which is to bring a modicum of freedom as an antidote to nihilism—we can, and will, prevail.

Note

1. James Q. Wilson, Foreword, in *The Essential Neoconservative Reader,* ed. Mark Gerson (Reading, MA: Addison-Wesley, 1996), viii.

Acknowledgments

As we set out to gather, authenticate, and reproduce the landmark speeches included in this volume, several individuals and institutions provided us with meaningful support. Chief among these was the editor of the Texas A&M University Press Presidential Rhetoric Series, Martin J. Medhurst. One of the premiere scholars in the field of presidential rhetoric, Marty's sage counsel proved invaluable. Thanks also go to his colleague, Texas A&M University Press Editor-in-Chief, Mary Lenn Dixon, for her dedication and professionalism.

We wish to thank the Hoover Institution on War, Revolution, and Peace at Stanford University and its director, John Raisian; the Earhart Foundation; and Barton A. Stebbins and his trustee, Donald W. Crowell, for their continued financial support. We would also like to thank Bainbridge College and the Bainbridge College Foundation for providing grant monies for the completion of this project. Thanks also to Ron Robinson of Young America's Foundation for his encouragement of this project.

The gathering of speech transcripts, video recordings, and other resources was made easier by several sources, all of whom we wish to thank. Michelle Easton and Lisa De Pasquale of The Clare Boothe Luce Policy Institute were instrumental in tracking down copies of Mrs. Luce's orations. One of these speeches had been previously published by The Human Life Foundation, which was kind enough to allow us to republish it here. The Yale University Library assisted with verifying details surrounding William F. Buckley's Class Day Oration. Moreover, Mr. Buckley kindly granted permission to reprint his speech, as did Charles Krauthammer, Newt Gingrich, and Phyllis Schlafly.

Finally, we wish to extend a special thanks to Katie Hall and our student research assistant, Jessica Schneider. Both provided invaluable assistance gathering research materials, editing documents, and aiding with the transcription of speech texts. Their attention to detail and commitment to the project made this book possible.

Index

Addams, Jane, 70

African-Americans, inequality of, 24

Aid to Dependent Children Program, 48

America: allies and, 147; Bush, George W., on, 130; changes of, 24–25; deficiencies/freedom/ prosperity in, 18–19, 33–38; democratic globalism and, 153–54; economy of, 73, 74–76; federal government and, 76; foreign policy and, 141, 144, 148–49, 153–54; greatness of, 84–85; international legitimacy and, 146; isolationism and, 143–44; Kennedy, Paul, on, 141–42; Krauthammer on, 142–43; liberal internationalism and, 150; monuments/symbols of, 79–80; morals of, 62–64, 69–72, 86, 88–89; people of, 77–78; September 11, 2001 and, 131, 136–38, 157; terrorism/war and, 131–36; de Tocqueville on, 84; UN and, 147; unilateralism and, 152; as unipolar power, 140, 141–43, 148, 150–52, 156–57, 158–59; Warren on, 78

American conservative movement: Absolute Truth and, 1; anticommunism and, 10; Chambers and, 10; critical moments in, 2; ideological content of, 1; Kirk/Weaver/Hayek/ Kristol and, 2; Nash on, 1–2; WFB and, 14

American Enterprise Institute, Irving Kristol Award and, 139

Annan, Kofi, 146

anticommunism: American conservative movement and, 10; Chambers and, 12–13

Area Redevelopment Agency, 46

Armed Ship bill, 23

Balz, Dan, 129

Beamer, Todd, 130

Beard, Charles, 17

Biden, Joseph, 145

Bierce, Ambrose,149

bin Laden, Osama, 156; Taliban and, 132

biography: of Buckley, 14–16; of Bush, Barbara, 105–106; of Bush, George W., 128–30; of Chambers, 9–10; of Dirksen, 20–21; of Gingrich, 111–12, 115; of Goldwater, 30–31; of Krauthammer, 139–41; of Luce, 55–57; of Reagan, 41–42, 73–74, 81–82; of Schlafly, 94–96

Blair, Tony, 153, 154

Bonior, Dave, 117

Buchanan, Pat, 144

Buckley, William F., Jr. (WFB), 3, 14–19; American conservative movement and, 14; biography of, 14–16; Chambers and, 10; governmental change and, 7; Jacoby on, 15; Presidential Medal of Freedom and, 15; Reagan on, 14

Bush, Barbara, 3, 4, 105–10; biography of, 105–106; on human connection, 108–109; on identity, 107, 108

Bush, George W., 4, 112, 141, 154; biography of, 128–30; call to nations and, 135–36; on Muslims, 134; on September 11, 2001, 136–37; on terrorism/war, 131–36, 138; on United States/Great Britain, 153; Zarefsky on, 129

Caesar, Augustus, on marriage/divorce, 68
Carter, Jimmy, 63, 71, 81
Chambers, Whittaker, 4, 41, 82, 92; American conservative movement and, 10; anticommunism and, 12–13; biography of, 9–10; Communist Party and, 3, 5, 9, 11–13; as conservative icon, 10; WFB/Hiss and, 10
Chemical Weapons Convention, Biden on, 145
Child Abuse in the Classroom (Schlafly), on moral dilemmas, 100
"Child Abuse in the Classroom" (Schlafly), 94–104
Choate, Joseph, 27
A Choice Not an Echo (Schlafly), 94
Churchill, Winston, 78
Cicero, on hypocrisy, 62
Civil Rights Act of 1964, 5; call of cloture on, 22–29; Dirksen and, 21–29; formation of, 22–23; LBJ and, 21; political parties and, 25–26
Clark (Senator), on liberalism, 44
Clay, Henry, 116
Clinton, Bill, 144–45
The Color Purple (Walker), 107–108
communism, 13, 35–36; Luce on, 56; Reagan and, 81–82, 91–93; totalitarianism and, 11, 82; WFB on, 17–18
Communist Party, 117; Chambers and, 3, 5, 9, 11–13; Goldwater on, 6; "Mother Bloor" and, 12
Confucius, 59, 61
Congressional Medal of Honor, 24
conservative(s): Chambers as, 10; compassionate, 128; governmental

change and, 7, 18, 39–40; higher power and, 3–4, 34; individual freedom/private property and, 5, 38, 45–47, 51, 77; Kirk on, 3, 4–5, 6, 7; man's will and, 6; moral equality and, 4–5, 26, 33–34; neoconservatism v., 140; proliferating life and, 4; rhetoric of, 2–7. See also American conservative movement
The Conservative Intellectual Movement in America (Nash), 1–2
The Conservative Mind (Kirk), 2
Constitution, 28; civil rights and, 23–24; Fifteenth Amendment to, 24; First Amendment of, 86–87, 99, 100, 101, 103; Fourteenth Amendment to, 24; Fulbright on, 44; Nineteenth Amendment to, 27; Sixteenth Amendment to, 27; Thirteenth Amendment to, 24
Constitutional Convention, Franklin and, 126–27
"The Contract with America" (Gingrich), 111–27
"The Controversy Ends Here" (Bush, B.), 105–10
Coolidge, Calvin, Chambers supporter of, 9
Coulter, Ann, 95–96

Declaration of Independence, 26, 79, 86; Lincoln and, 28
DeLay, Tom, 117
Dellums, Ron, 118
democratic globalism: America and, 153–54; liberal internationalism and, 155; realism and, 155; unipolarity and, 158; Wilson, Woodrow, and, 154–55
Democratic Party: failures of, 35; Gephardt on, 122; on Iraq war, 146–47
Department of Education, 100
The Devil's Dictionary (Bierce), 149
Dingell, John, 113
Dirksen, Everett, 5, 20–29; biography

of, 20–21; Civil Rights Act of 1964 and, 21–29; German ancestry of, 20, 21; Mansfield on, 21; Republican Party and, 20; as senator, 20–21

Distinguished Service Cross, 24

domestic society: authority and, 149; international system and, 149

Eagle Forum, ERA and, 95

Economic Interpretation of the Constitution (Beard), 17

Ehlers, Vern, 125

Eisenhower, Dwight D. (Ike), 31, 35; Luce and, 56

Emerson, Bill, 126

Equal Rights Amendment (ERA), passage of, 94–95

ERA. *See* Equal Rights Amendment

EU. *See* European Union

European Union (EU), international system and, 149

"Evil Empire" (Reagan), 3–4, 81–93, 154

"Extremism in the Defense of Liberty Is No Vice" (Goldwater), 31–40

Federal Housing Administration (FHA), 46

Feinstein, Dianne, 129

FHA. *See* Federal Housing Administration

Firing Line (show), WFB and, 15

"The First Inaugural" (Reagan), 73–80

Foreign Intelligence Advisory Board, 56

Franklin, Benjamin, Constitutional Convention and, 126–27

Fulbright, J. William, on Constitution, 44

Fulghum, Robert, on diversity, 107

Garfield, James, 27

Gephardt, Dick, 112, 116, 122, 131; Gingrich and, 119–20, 126

Gingrich, Newt, 5, 111–27; on being a whip, 117–18; biography of, 111–12, 115; on budgets, 120, 121–22, 122, 125; on family, 118–19, 123–24; Gephardt and, 119–20, 126; on reforms, 119, 120, 125; for republican takeover, 111–12; on republican/democratic party, 122; on Rhodes, 114; on voting, 119

Giuliani, Rudolph, 137

God and Man at Yale (Buckley), 14, 15–16

Goethe, on morals, 71–72

Goldwater, Barry, 6; biography of, 30–31; character of, 51–52; on freedom/failures, 32–40; Johnson *v.*, 31; Reagan as supporter of, 41–54; Republican Party and, 30–40; on stable government, 38–39; Thomas on, 50; on world government, 35–36

GOP. *See* Republican Party

Gore, Al, 121, 129

government: change of, 7, 18, 39–40; morals and, 62; stable, 38–39; taxes/spending and, 42–43, 47–48, 50, 75

Grady, Henry W., on new South, 25

Grunderson, Steve, 117

Hamilton, Alexander, 53

Hayakawa, Sam, 99; on education, 98

Hayek, F. A., 2

Hazlitt, Henry, on hypocrisy, 62

Health and Human Services Department, Rehabilitation Act of 1973 and, 87–88

Hilbert, David, 157

Hippocratic Oath, 63

Hiss, Alger, 12; Chambers and, 10

Hobbesian world, Lockean world and, 148–49

Holmes, John Haynes, 59

Hoover, Herbert, 31; on Whig party, 25

House Un-American Activities Committee, Chambers and, 5, 9, 10–13

Howard, George, 138

Hull, Cordell, on new world, 148
Huxley, Thomas, 60
Hyde, Henry, abortions and, 88

"I Broke Away from the Communist
Party" (Chambers), 9–13
Ike. *See* Eisenhower, Dwight D.
International Congress of Mathematicians, Hilbert and, 157
international system: domestic society
and, 149; EU and, 149; power in,
152; realism and, 149–50
Irving Kristol Award, Krauthammer
and, 140
"Is the New Morality Destroying America?" (Luce), 55–72; on hypocrisy,
62; on marriage, 65–70; on sexual
morality, 6–7, 56, 64–71; on universal morality, 59, 61, 65, 66–68; on
virtues, 61–62
isolationism: America and, 143–44;
unipolarity and, 158

Jacoby, Jeff, 15
Jefferson, Thomas, 79; on equality, 26,
29; on God, 84
Johnson, Lyndon Baines (LBJ): Civil
Rights Act of 1964 and, 21; Goldwater *v.*, 31

Kant, Immanuel, Moral Law and, 59
Kennan, George, 154
Kennedy, John F., 21–22, 144, 153
Kennedy, Paul, 141–42
Kerry, John, 144
Kirk, Russell, 2, 3, 4–5, 6, 7
Krauthammer, Charles, 139–59; on
America, 142–43; biography of, 139–
41; for democracy/liberty, 140–41; Pulitzer
Prize or Distinguished Commentary
and, 140; on September 11, 2001, 157
Kristol, Irving, 2, 152; neoconservatism and, 140
Kyoto Protocol, 146

Lamb, Brian, 116
Law of Unintended Consequences, 140
Lawrence of Arabia (Lean), 142
LBJ. *See* Johnson, Lyndon Baines
Lean, David, 142
Lenin, Vladimir, 11, 89
Lewis, C. S., 4, 82, 91
liberal internationalism, 144; America
and, 150; Clinton and, 144–45;
democratic globalism and, 155;
Iraq war and, 147; multilateralism
and, 146, 147–48; unipolarity and,
158
Liberman, Joseph, 129
Life (magazine), 9, 55
Lincoln, Abraham, 21, 39, 80, 83; on
change, 25; Declaration of Independence and, 28; equality and, 28;
politics and, 17
Lockean world, Hobbesian world and,
148–49
Luce, Clare Boothe, 6–7; biography
of, 55–57; Eisenhower and, 56; as
feminist, 56–57; on morals, 58–72;
Reagan and, 56

Mandela, Nelson, 118
Mansfield, Mike, 21
Marx, Karl, 11
McCarthy, Joseph, 10
Michel, Bob, 112, 114–15
Miller, Bill, 31
Mondale, Walter, 139
moral(s): of America, 62–64, 69–72,
86, 88–89; Carter on, 71; crime
rate and, 64; dilemmas of, 100,
101–103; equality, 4–5, 26, 33–34;
Goethe on, 71–72; Golden Rule
and, 61; government and, 62;
honesty and, 60; Luce on, 58–72;
Ruskin on, 59; sexual, 64–71,
85, 101–103; Spencer on, 60–61;
suasion, 145–46; training of,
67–68; universal, 59, 61, 65, 66–68;
universal *v.* new *v.* traditional, 59;

Wilson, Woodrow, on, 60; Wolf on, 118. *See also* sexual morality, universal
Morgenthau, Hans, 154
"Mother Bloor," 12
Muggeridge, Malcolm, 69
multilateralism: Clinton and, 145; liberal internationalism and, 146, 147–48; unilateralism and, 152

Nash, George H., 1–2
National Association of Evangelicals: annual convention of, 3–4; Reagan's address to, 82–93
National Labor Relations Board, 12
National Review (NR), WFB and, 15
neoconservatism, 3, 10, 139–40; conservatives *v.,* 140; Kristol and, 140
New York City Board of Education, 103; legal services of, 4; Schlafly and, 4
New York School Board. *See* New York City Board of Education
Newman, Dorsey, 114
9/11. *See* September 11, 2001
1964 Republican National Convention, 6; presidential acceptance speech at, 31–40
Nixon, Richard, 31, 106
NR. See National Review

OAS. *See* Organization of American States
Office of Homeland Security, 135
Olasky, Marvin, 112, 123
Organization of American States (OAS), Kristol on, 152
"Our Mission and Our Moment" (Bush, G. W.), 128–38; Balz/Woodward/Feinstein/Liberman on, 129; response to, 129–30; on terrorism/war, 131–36, 138

Pataki, George, 137
Pendleton Act, 27

Penn, William, on God, 84
People for the American Way, 97
The Portable Abraham Lincoln, 117
preemption: doctrine of, 151; intelligence for, 151; of WMDs, 151
Presidential Medal of Freedom: Luce and, 56; WFB and, 15
Protection of Pupil Rights Amendment, Hayakawa and, 99
Pulitzer Prize for Distinguished Commentary, Krauthammer and, 140

al- Qaeda, 131–32; war against, 134

Reagan, Ronald, 4, 14, 31, 73–80, 97, 111, 154; on American people, 77–78, 85–88; biography of, 41–42, 73–74, 81–82; communism and, 81–82, 91–93; on conservative banner, 1; on continuity/change, 73–74; on farm economy, 45–46; on freedom, 78–79; as Goldwater supporter, 41–54; on government planning/programs, 44–49, 73–74; governmental change and, 7; on Kirk, 3; Luce and, 56; on Michel, 114–15; on nuclear freeze, 90, 92; political affiliation of, 2–3; on prayer/God, 82–84; religion and, 82–84, 86, 88–89, 92–93; Roosevelt and, 41; on socialism, 49–51; on Soviet Union, 89–90; on taxes/government spending, 42–43, 47–48, 50, 75; on war/peace, 52–54, 82
realism: democratic globalism and, 155; foreign policy and, 148–49; international system and, 149–50; limits of, 152–53; unipolarity and, 158
Rehabilitation Act of 1973, 87–88
religion: God and, 82–84; high power and, 34; higher power and, 3–4; Reagan and, 82–84, 86, 88–89, 92–93; Ruskin on, 59; schools, public, and, 100, 101, 103–104

Republican Party, 2; Dirksen and, 20; Gingrich and, 111–12; Goldwater and, 30–40; Lincoln on, 39; peace/success of, 35; reforms by, 119; shift of, 31–40, 42–54. *See also* republicanism

republicanism, 18; cause for, 34–35, 39–40

Rhodes, John, 114

Ridge, Tom, 135

Roosevelt, Franklin Delano, 10, 122, 141; Reagan and, 41

Rousseau, Jean Jacques, on family, 65

Ruskin, John, on religion/morals, 59

Schectman, Morris, 124

Schlafly, Phyllis, 4, 94–104; on Alabama textbook case, 100–102, 104; biography of, 94–96; Coulter on, 95–96; on Jaffree case, 101–102; on public schools, 96–104

schools, public: curriculum of, 100; moral dilemmas in, 100; reading and, 98; religion and, 100, 101, 103–104; taxpayers and, 97

Screwtape Letters (Lewis), 91

Senate Judiciary Committee, 22; moral issues and, 26–28

September 11, 2001: America and, 131, 136–38, 157; Bush, George W., on, 136–37; enemy behind, 156; Krauthammer on, 157; world response to, 131; World Trade Center and, 131

"Sex, Drugs and AIDS," 103

sexual morality, universal: authority/responsibility and, 66–67; education/training and, 67–68; faithfulness and, 67; welfare/protection and, 66

Shaw, Bernard, 65–66

Simon, Sidney, 99

Social Security, 48–49, 121

socialism, 5, 141; Reagan on, 49–51

Solzhenitsyn, Aleksandr, 63

speeches, rhetorical artistry/conservative principles of, 2

Spencer, Herbert, on morals, 60–61

Stalin, Joseph, 9

Strategic Defense Initiative, 82

Stuart Mill, John, on moral training, 67–68

Student Bill of Rights, 103

Taliban: bin Laden and, 132; United States demands for, 132–33

terrorism: America and, 131–36; Bush, George W., on, 131–36, 138

Thatcher, Margaret, 96, 153

Thomas, Norman, 50

Time (magazine), 55, 140; on Dirksen, 21

"A Time for Choosing" (Reagan), 42–54

"The Time Has Come" (Dirksen), on Civil Rights Act of 1964, 21–29

de Tocqueville, Alexis, 84; on society, 116

"Today We Are Educated Men" (Buckley), 14–19

totalitarianism, 91; Arab-Islamic, 154, 156; communism and, 11, 82

The Tragedy of American Compassion (Olasky), 112, 123

Truman Doctrine, 154

Truman, Harry, 141, 144

UN. *See* United Nations

unilateralism, multilateralism and, 152

"A Unipolar World" (Krauthammer), 139–59

United Nations (UN), America and, 147

United States. *See* America

Values Clarification (Simon), 99

Veterans Administration, 46

Walker, Alice, 105, 107–108

war: America and, 131–36; Bush, George W., on, 131–36, 138; Iraq,

146–47; against al-Qaeda, 134;
Reagan on, 52–54, 82
Warren, Joseph, 78
Washington, George, 79, 84
weapons of mass destruction (WMDs),
145–46, 151
Weaver, Richard M., 2
Wellesley College, commencement ad-
dress for, 4, 106–10
WFB. *See* Buckley, William F., Jr.
Whig party, 26; Hoover on, 25
Wilson, James Q., on neoconservatism,
139–40
Wilson, Woodrow, 141; democratic
globalism and, 154–55; on morals, 60

WMDs. *See* weapons of mass destruction
Wolf, Frank, 118
Woodward, Bob, 129
Working without a Net (Schectman),
caring *v.* caretaking in, 124
World Trade Center, 4, 138; September
11, 2001 and, 131

Yale University, 105, 128; class day
oration at, 16–19; enlightenment from, 18–19; prestige of,
16–17

Zarefsky, David, 129